# Using Music in Children of Divorce Groups:

## A Session-by-Session Manual for Counselors

Janice L. DeLucia-Waack, PhD

To Be Used in Conjunction With
Dan Conley's "If You Believe In You" Tape

Using Music in Children of Divorce Groups:
A Session-by-Session Manual for Counselors

10 9 8 7 6 5 4 3 2 1

**American Counseling Association**
5999 Stevenson Avenue
Alexandria, VA 22304

Director of Publications
Carolyn C. Baker

Production Manager
Bonny Gaston

Copy Editor
Sharon Doyle

**Cover Art by Lizzy Rockwell**
**Cover design by Kim Dibona**

Library of Congress Cataloging-in-Publication Data

DeLucia-Waack, Janice L.
   Using music in Children of Divorce groups : a session-by-session manual for
counselors / by Janice L. DeLucia-Waack.
       p.   cm.
   Includes bibliographical references (p. 109).
   ISBN 1-55620-176-1 (alk. paper)
   1. Music therapy for children.   2. Children of divorce—Counseling of.
3. Group counseling for children.   I. Title.

ML3920.D35   2000
362.82′9486—dc21

                                                        00-045411

## User's Guide to ACA Reproducible Books

As part of our general effort to provide educational materials that are as practical and economical as possible, we have designated this publication as a "reproducible book." The designation means that purchase of the book includes purchase of the right to limited reproduction of all pages on which this symbol appears: 📑

We grant to individual purchasers of this book the right to make sufficient copies of reproducible pages for use by all students of a single teacher or counselor. This permission is limited to a single teacher or counselor and does not apply to entire schools, school systems, or organizations, so institutions purchasing the book should pass the permission on to a single teacher or counselor. Copying of the book or its parts for resale is prohibited.

Any questions regarding this policy or requests to purchase further reproduction rights should be addressed to Rights and Permissions Editor, American Counseling Association, 5999 Stevenson Avenue, Alexandria, VA 22304; 703-823-9800 ext. 249.

# Table of Contents

# Dedication

To Jim, Kelsey, and Matthew, who are my family and the loves of my life;

To Dan, Phyllis, Kelly, and Cory, who through their music
and experiences made this idea come alive; and

To all the school counselors who warmly embraced the idea
of music in children of divorce groups.

# About the Author and Songwriter

**Janice L. DeLucia-Waack, PhD,** is currently the editor of the *Journal for Specialists in Group Work* and an associate professor in the Counseling, Educational, and School Psychology Department at the State University of New York at Buffalo. She is the program director of the School Counseling Program and also teaches graduate-level group work courses. Janice has authored more than 30 articles, books, and book chapters related to group work, supervision, and eating disorders. Her counseling and research interests include children of divorce, supervision, use of activities in group work, relationship issues, and eating disorders.

**Dan Conley** is currently a middle school counselor in the Greenwich, Connecticut school district, with more than 20 years of experience. In addition to working as a school counselor, Dan's experience with children includes working as a principal at a special needs elementary school and as a counselor in a school for deaf children. As a second career, Dan is a singer and songwriter of children's and adult music. He has written several songs for two of the Olsen twins' albums, including **"I Am A Kid,"** **"It Is Not Logical,"** and **"Nothing to Do."** Dan currently has two albums of his own out for children, **"Yes, Yes, Yes"** and **"If You Believe In You."** His album **"If You Believe In You"** focuses specifically on self-esteem and issues related to children of divorce. For more information about Dan and his music, contact him at 7 Wakerobin Road, Norwalk, Connecticut 06851 or conley@optonline.net.

# Introduction: How to Use This Manual

## INTRODUCTION

**Divorce Is a Major Issue for Children.** Parental divorce is the issue of most concern for elementary school children (Nelson & Crawford, 1990). Approximately one million divorces are granted each year in the United States, and one third of all children experience parental divorce before age 18 (Garvin, Leber, & Kalter, 1991). Furthermore, it is projected that 40% of all American children will be affected by parental divorce by the time they reach the age of 18 (Barker, Brinkman, & Deardoff, 1995). Divorce has long-term implications for both parents and children.

Research suggests that children of divorce are more likely to have problems at school and in relationships as they mature. Garvin et al. (1991) found that compared with children of maritally intact parents, children of divorced parents had higher rates of depression, sexual acting out, substance abuse, conduct disorders, school problems, and delinquent behavior. Children of divorce have also been reported to exhibit higher levels of hostility and aggression (Spigelman & Spigelman, 1991). Furthermore, Mulholland, Watt, Philpott, and Sarlin (1991) suggested that differences in academic performance for children of divorce could not be attributed to differences in social class or intellectual ability. Amato and Keith (1991), in a meta-analysis of 92 studies, compared children of divorce in single-parent families with children living in continuously intact families on measures of well-being. Children of divorce scored lower than children living in intact families, with the median effect size being .14 of a standard deviation.

**Children of Divorce Have Different Needs.** Consequently, children of divorce have different and/or additional needs than children with intact families. It is important to provide children of divorce with information about separation, divorce, visitation, parental fighting, parental dating, stepparents, and remarriage (Cebollero, Cruise, & Stollak, 1987; Rosenstein-Manner, 1990). Children of divorce often need a safe place to talk and to process information related to the divorce. They need to be able to normalize their experiences, clarify divorce-related concerns, receive support, realize that they are not alone in their feelings or experiences, and discuss ways to cope with the changes in their lives. Thus, treatment for children of divorce should assist them in sharing and developing coping skills and behaviors to deal with situations related to the divorce.

**Group Counseling Is the Treatment of Choice for Children of Divorce.** Guldner and O'Connor (1991) stated that "where possible, group therapy for dealing with problems of children of divorce is the treatment of choice" (p. 184). Group counseling theory emphasizes the usefulness of a group setting in helping members to feel less isolated, to connect with and learn from others, to receive peer validation and support, and to normalize experiences (Gladding, 1991). Kalter (1998) suggested several reasons for using group work with children of divorce. Being in a group allows youngsters to interact with peers around divorce-related issues; acknowledges their inner reactions and helps them realize that they are widely shared, understandable, and normal; provides a source of peer support, especially when traditional family sources of support are less available; and provides children with a sense of safety in numbers. Group work, both in schools and in agencies, has been an extremely popular and efficient method of providing treatment for children of divorce (Bornstein, Bornstein, & Walters, 1988; Crosbie-Burnett & Newcomer, 1990; Gwynn & Brantley, 1987; Howard & Scherman, 1990; Rosenstein-Manner, 1990).

It is important to acknowledge the differences in working with children versus adults, particularly in group work. Children have shorter attention spans, they are more likely to project their feelings onto others, and they have much less control over their situation and their environment. Thus, different techniques must be used to ensure that children participate fully and in interventions that suit their developmental level.

**Creative Arts, Particularly Music, Are Effective With Children.** Counseling and psychoeducational interventions for children of divorce should assist these children in sharing and developing coping skills and behaviors to deal with situations related to divorce. Creativity in activities, particularly singing, dancing, and music, is a way for children to identify and express feelings and to brainstorm and practice new behaviors and coping skills (DeLucia-Waack, 1996; Gladding, 1998). Specific techniques aimed at creativity, such as the use of music in group sessions, are often advocated but have not been previously applied to groups for children of divorce.

Gladding (1998) suggested that creative arts, such as music, in counseling are beneficial for a number of reasons: (a) to experience the connectedness between mind and body, (b) to increase energy flow, (c) to focus on goals, (d) to increase creativity, (e) to establish a new sense of self, (f) to provide concrete interventions that are beneficial, (g) to provide insight, and (h) to promote socialization and cooperation. Music is particularly important when trying to help children to express their feelings. Music also helps to link people and gives them a common denominator with which to relate. Children, in particular, relate to music because they may not have the vocabulary to express certain feelings and the words to a song may provide a way for them to express themselves.

## PURPOSE AND RATIONALE FOR THIS MANUAL

The purpose of this manual is to provide school counselors and counselors in agency settings with a very specific, hands-on, concrete set of materials for them to use in group work with children of divorce. The goals are to describe a comprehensive psychoeducational group work program with which counselors can assess the specific needs of children of divorce, to provide a psychoeducational group for these children on the basis of their specific needs, and to assess the outcome of the group. Music has been incorporated into this group work program to increase children's integration of the skills learned in the group and application of the skills to their lives outside of the group. Each package consists of a leader manual for the counselor as well as seven tapes of **"If You Believe In You"** by singer and songwriter Dan Conley to use as the music part of the group.

**Music Is Used to Reinforce What Has Been Learned in Group Sessions.** In this manual, music has been added to traditional methods and interventions for children of divorce groups to serve a variety of functions. Music is used to encourage children to express their feelings, problem solve, and brainstorm coping strategies. It is also used in group sessions to introduce topics, get the sessions started, change topics, and end the sessions on an upbeat note. Children participating in these groups are expected to take the tapes home to further reinforce what they learn and experience in group sessions. Music serves as a concrete reminder and reinforcer of what they have learned in group. The tapes provide an opportunity for the children to sing outside of group when they feel sad or lonely or when something happens related to the divorce or their parents. The songs serve as a reminder of the coping strategies that have been discussed in group and also help children feel better.

**Prepared Lesson Plans for Each Group Session Are Easy to Follow and Use.** There are several reasons for the creation of this manual. First, school counselors are actively leading children of divorce groups in great numbers, and thus, there is a need for resource materials for these groups. The second reason is related to the first and is perhaps the most important reason for the creation of this manual. School counselors are very busy and have many demands on their time. They often don't have time to read the literature and then design materials for children of divorce groups. This manual provides counselors with materials to use in children of divorce groups that are based on current theory and research in the field of counseling and group work.

**Processing Activities Are Described to Facilitate Discussion and Application of the Material.** Third, the most common mistake made in group work is insufficient processing of activities. It is not enough to give group counselors a stimulus; they need guidelines about how to facilitate productive discussion with group members (Jacobs, Harvill, & Masson, 1988). This manual provides specific focus and processing questions for each activity that relate to the child, the group, and the application of the skills discussed.

**Music Is an Effective Intervention With Children.** Fourth, creative arts, specifically music, are very effective in working with children and particularly children in groups. Music is a natural medium that is easily accessed and readily accepted by children.

This music is specifically written for children of divorce by an experienced school counselor. The voices on the tape are of a father, daughter, son, and stepmother. Dan is the father, and Jean is the mother. They separated before both of their children, Kelly and Cory, started school. Phyllis, the stepmother, has been in the children's lives since soon after the divorce. This scenario provides the children with a chance to talk about what they would be feeling when they listen to the voices on the tape. Young children often project their thoughts and feelings onto characters in books, plays, and songs. These songs are a good place for them to do this.

This book is unique in two ways: First, it provides counselors with a comprehensive plan of how to lead children of divorce groups, and second, music is a key component of the groups.

## USE OF MUSIC WITH CHILDREN OF DIVORCE GROUPS

**Music Is a Powerful Medium.**  Music is a powerful medium that works well with most children. Music also helps to link people and gives them a common denominator with which to relate. Children, in particular, relate to music because they may not have the vocabulary to express certain feelings and the words to a song may provide a way for them to express themselves. Music is a natural medium that is easily accessed and readily accepted by children. The song **"Divorce"** identifies several of the thoughts and feelings that children may typically have when they find out that their parents are getting divorced or separated (i.e., disbelief, anger, sadness, shock, hurt). **"Is It My Fault?"** focuses on the irrational fear that children may have that they somehow caused the divorce, whereas **"I Tried"** expresses the magical and wishful thinking that children often have about their parents getting back together again.

**Songs Help to Identify Important Themes and Issues.**  Songs are particularly useful in terms of helping children of divorce to identify potential thoughts and feelings through the concept of displacement (Beech Acres Aring Institute, 1993). Children are able to listen to a song and then discuss what the child who sang the song (or the person who wrote it) might have been feeling or thinking. This "one step removed" technique identifies potential feelings and thoughts without attaching them to a specific group member, something that can be threatening for a child. Such a technique also helps to normalize some of the children's experiences as they realize that others have similar thoughts and feelings about divorce. The song **"Divorce"** lists other children whose parents have separated or divorced and leads into an activity in which the group can list all the people they know whose parents are divorced, including celebrities, TV and movie characters, and their friends and family, to normalize the experience of divorce. The song **"Is It My Fault?"** facilitates the "one step removed" technique in which the children can then discuss what Cory (who is singing the song) might be feeling when he is singing, what he might have done that he thinks caused the divorce, and then how realistic or unrealistic his thoughts are about how the divorce occurred. Because the children are talking about Cory (but are probably projecting their feelings and fears), it is safe to express the feelings and fears, and the group leader and other members can indirectly confront and challenge some of the irrational beliefs that the children may hold about how divorce occurs.

**Songs Serve a Variety of Purposes In and Outside of Group Sessions.**  Songs can serve a variety of purposes within and outside of a children of divorce group. Within a session, songs can be used to introduce a topic; begin a discussion; lead to an activity; channel energy; suggest potential thoughts, feelings, or new behaviors; or end a session with positive affect. In addition, transfer of learning outside of the group is difficult for younger children and often requires a concrete stimulus to remind them of their newly learned coping skills. Music, specifically songs, may serve as such a stimulus for children. At home, children may listen to songs as a way to cope with distressing feelings and/or remind them of strategies that they have discussed in group. **"If You Believe In You"** is a very calming song that children may listen to and sing along with at home when they get upset and need to calm down. Listening to **"Everybody Needs A Friend"** reminds children that they need to talk to their friends when they are upset to express their feelings and try to figure out solutions to their problems. **"Bad Mood"** reinforces that everybody has a bad day and that one needs to find ways to get out of bad moods.

## THE MUSIC BY DAN CONLEY

There are a variety of songs that can be used in children of divorce groups. Some songs on the accompanying tape have been written specifically for children of divorce, whereas others have been written as psychoeducational interventions for children in general. Dan Conley, an accomplished children's songwriter and a school counselor with more than 20 years of experience, wrote all of these songs specifically as counseling and therapeutic interventions. On the tape **"If You Believe In You"** (Conley, 1994), four songs focus specifically on the issues that children of divorce are experiencing: **"Divorce," "I Tried," "Is It My Fault?,"** and **"I Worry."** The other eight songs on the tape focus more generally on the issues of self-esteem, expression of feelings, and need for support from friends: **"And I Need A Lot Of Love," "Perfect People," "Casey The Clown," "I Am A Kid," "Bad Mood," "So Am I," "Everybody Needs A Friend,"** and **"If You Believe In You."** For example, the phrase "Life is tough . . . and so am I" from the song **"So Am I"** reminds children that they are strong and they can face stress and still go on. **"Everybody Needs A Friend"** is a reminder that when a person feels sad, it helps to talk to someone. **"I Worry"** helps children examine their worries and decide which they must let go of and which they must let parents (and other adults) worry about. **"Is It My Fault?"** addresses the irrational belief that children often have that they somehow caused the divorce.

This manual suggests a framework for leading counseling and psychoeducational groups for children of divorce using music as the major intervention. The recommendations are based on an extensive review of the literature related to children of divorce, group work for children, and counseling for children, in addition to six years of counseling practice leading psychoeducational and counseling groups for children of divorce with music.

## GOALS OF THIS GROUP WORK PROGRAM

The general goals of this group work program are psychoeducational in terms of providing information and new skills to deal with a stressful situation in children's lives. The focus is on creating a safe environment for children to discuss feelings and experiences and develop new coping skills related to their issues from the divorce. Central to this group is the use of music as an in-group strategy to keep the children focused and interested and outside of group as a coping strategy and a reminder of what has been learned in group. Specific goals for psychoeducational and counseling-oriented children of divorce groups focus on coping with the reality of the divorce situation as well as the feelings elicited by it.

*Goal 1:* **To help children gain an accurate picture of the divorce process through discussion and information.** It is important to provide children of divorce with information about separation, divorce, custody, visitation, parental fighting, parental dating, stepparents, blended families, and remarriage (Cebollero et al., 1987). Early sessions focus on defining words such as separation, divorce, and custody. Wilcoxon and Magnusom's (1999) article is a good resource with specific definitions of these and related terms. Later sessions focus on how families deal with issues of visitation, parental dating, and blended families.

*Goal 2:* **To normalize the common experiences and feelings around divorce.** Children need a safe place to talk about their thoughts, feelings, and experiences with others, both adults and children, who are not involved in the divorce or their family. It is important that they learn that their situation is not unique and that other children also live with one parent (or other family members) and have parents who do not get along. They also need to share their experiences related to divorce, such as how they found out about the divorce and what their visits are like with the noncustodial parents, in a nonjudgmental environment. Groups create a place where children can receive peer support and validation for what they experience and feel.

*Goal 3:* **To provide a safe and supportive place to talk about divorce-related concerns.** It is helpful in early sessions to have children draw pictures of what their families look like. This process helps children share about the divorce and also connect with each other on similarities. Sentence completion exercises such as "The most frustrating part of divorce for me is . . . ," "I would like Dad (Mom) to . . . ," and "One thing that has changed for the better is . . . " also help to begin and structure discussions about concerns related to the divorce.

*Goal 4:* **To help children label, understand, and express feelings about the divorce.** Young children may often deny their feelings of loss over the separation. Discussion of these feelings, particularly about the loss of a parent through divorce, is very important. Children need to be able to express the anger, fear, and sadness that they may be experiencing. Because the divorce or separation has significantly changed the constellation of their family, they need to mourn the loss of their family of origin as it was or the way they would like it to be. They also need help focusing on their feelings of guilt; children often feel responsible for the divorce in some way. Disloyalty is another feeling that arises for children of divorce; they may feel that they are being asked to choose one parent over another or that if they make certain choices, then the other parent will be angry or hurt or may leave them. Early exercises in group focus on the identification of feelings through the use of aids such as feeling charts and feeling charades. Later, activities that act out feelings behaviorally are useful to help children learn about and focus on their feelings, normalize expression of both positive and negative emotions, and practice expressing feelings in different situations and to different people.

*Goal 5*: **To assist children in developing new coping skills to deal with the feelings and situations experienced as a result of the divorce.** The skills that children already know may be too limited or overtaxed to deal with the multitude of issues surrounding the divorce. Techniques that may be useful in this process include teaching and practicing communication, problem-solving, anger management, and conflict resolution skills. Communication and conflict resolution skills may be particularly useful around the issues of stepfamily problems, parental and sibling conflicts, and divided parental loyalty. Role-playing of relevant situations such as parental arguing, custody, and court scenarios helps children to understand difficulties, gain perspective, see others' viewpoints, and express their fears about potential situations, enabling them to identify new ways of coping.

*Goal 6*: **To use reality testing as an important focus of children of divorce groups.** Children, particularly young children, often have unrealistic fears and beliefs about what will happen as a result of the divorce. They may fear that both parents will stop loving them and/or will abandon them or that they have in some way caused the divorce by wishful thinking or something they did. Some of the irrational fears and thoughts can be dispelled through exercises in which a possible situation is described and the group is then asked to decide how likely it is that that situation could happen.

The last two goals focus on the future:

*Goal 7*: **To help children gain realistic and attainable dreams about their family life for the future.** They also need to gain a realistic perspective about how relationships work and what to expect in a relationship. Groups for children of divorce instill hope for the future when children see others changing and adapting to and even enjoying their new situation.

*Goal 8*: **To help the children focus on the positive aspects of their new family structure as well as the negative** (spending more time with the mother or father, less arguing between parents, seeing grandparents more, being closer to siblings, etc.).

## HOW THIS MANUAL WORKS

This manual is designed to serve as a resource guide. The needs of children in each children of divorce group will differ as will the strengths and limitations of the group counselor and the group setting. Thus, this manual is written to help counselors to design a children of divorce group specific to their population, goals, and time constraints.

**Chapter Topics.** The first chapter provides general guidelines about how to plan, lead, and evaluate children of divorce groups. Such issues as coleadership; preparation of leaders and members for group; recruitment, screening, and selection; group format and structure; parent, child, and agency consent; and assessment of group effectiveness and group process are discussed. Sample forms and assessment materials are included.

The second chapter focuses on introductory sessions of a group—starting the group, setting ground rules, and helping members to get to know each other and start to work together. Three introductory sessions are included. The third chapter begins by describing how to work with content sessions or the working stage of the group. Twenty-six content sessions follow. There are six sessions on the **divorce experience;** four on **feelings;** two on **communication skills;** one each on **parental fighting, maintaining parental relationships,** and **feeling caught in the middle;** two on **legal aspects;** three on **changes;** four on **parents' new partners;** and two on **stepfamilies.** At the end of chapter 3 is a table listing sessions by title and grouped by topic. Chapter 4 describes how to structure ending, or termination, sessions and includes three termination sessions. Chapter 5 focuses on possible adaptations of group sessions, activities, and the music. Appendix A contains a list of songs and the sessions they are used in. Appendix B provides sample forms and explanatory handouts, while Appendix C offers assessment forms that can help in monitoring the efficacy of the group work on an ongoing basis. The Association for Specialists in Group Work (ASGW) Professional Standards for the Training of Group Workers, Best Practice Guidelines, and Principles for Diversity-Competent Group Workers are included as additional information related to the field of group work as Appendixes D, E, and F, respectively. Suggestions for resources related to divorce, group work, and counseling in general are listed in Appendix G. Appendix H contains session planners to be used when planning children of divorce groups.

**Suggested Group Plans.** An informal poll of school counselors indicated that most of them led children of divorce groups for 6 to 8 sessions, suggesting 1 introductory session, 1 termination session, and 4 to 6 content sessions. Suggested outlines of sessions are included in Appendix H. Sample outlines for 8- and 12-session groups are also included in Appendix H as are planning sheets to customize a group based on topic and individual members' needs.

**Assessment of Children's Needs.** A counselor might also want to conduct an assessment of the individual needs and concerns of group members before deciding what sessions should be conducted. Sample assessment materials are provided to aid in this process in Appendix C. For example, school counselors might identify the following concerns as being most important to their group: feelings, the divorce experience, and feeling caught in the middle, and then, on the basis of this assessment, choose **Session**

**1-A: How Divorce Happened in My Family, Session I-B: Lots of Children Have Parents Who Are Divorced, Session 2-A: Feelings About the Divorce,** and **Session 6: Some Ways to Cope With Parents Who Don't Live Together** as content sessions. This procedure is particularly helpful when students have already received individual and/or group counseling related to divorce or when the group members have been dealing with their issues related to being children of divorce for a number of years.

*Chapter*

# 1

# Guidelines for Organizing a Children of Divorce Group

Although the general goals of children of divorce groups may be similar, each group will have its own specific goals, organization, and structure depending on the unique personalities and concerns of the group members. This chapter discusses key issues relevant to the planning, execution, and evaluation of children of divorce groups. First, pregroup planning decisions for children of divorce groups are identified. Next, strategies for screening, selection, and recruitment of group members are described. Strategies and instruments to assess the effectiveness and process of children of divorce groups are also suggested. Also discussed is how group counselors prepare to lead a group with regard to content, process, and possibly coleadership.

## STEP 1: PREGROUP DECISION MAKING

**Group Goals.** A group counselor must decide on the general goals for the children of divorce group prior to selection of group members and then can tailor the specific content after individual members of the group are identified. First, the counselor must decide if the group will be psychoeducational or counseling-oriented in its focus. For elementary school and early middle school students, psychoeducational groups are most appropriate because of their structure and focus on skill building. This manual provides a psychoeducational group work design. ASGW Professional Standards for the Training of Group Workers are included in Appendix D; they contain specific definitions of psychoeducational and counseling groups as well as guidelines for training and skills related to each specific type of group work. ASGW Best Practice Guidelines are included in Appendix E to suggest ethical behavior. ASGW Principles for Diversity-Competent Group Workers are included in Appendix F to address issues of diversity in group work.

Not all groups will focus on and/or accomplish all of the goals discussed in the introductory chapter. Specific group goals may be chosen by the leader on the basis of an interview with individual members about their concerns, a formal assessment of members' concerns, or group discussion and consensus about what issues should be focused on in the group. It is helpful to write out the goals as a first step toward planning the group for several reasons. First, all activities should be based on the specific goals. As a general guideline, at least one session should be spent on each goal or area of concern. For example, reasonable goals for a 6-week children of divorce group for 2nd and 3rd graders include gaining an accurate picture of the divorce process, normalizing the common experiences and feelings related to divorce, and providing a safe and supportive place to talk about divorce-related concerns. In each session outline that is provided later in the manual, the goals for that session are identified. Second, potential members, their parents, and any administrators who must give their approval should be told of the specific goals of the group.

**Gender Mix and Group Size.** On the basis of the goals of the group, a decision must be made as to how many children and of what gender the group will be comprised. Ideal group size varies according to the age of the children, beginning with 3 to 6 children in younger age groups, 5 to 7 children between ages 6 and 9, and up to 8 children in older age groups. Mixed-sex groups seem to work well until early middle school, when gender pressures set in. It is ultimately up to the style and experience of the counselor as to whether to lead mixed- or single-gender groups. Some counselors report the diversity in emotions and reactions in mixed groups enhances their effectiveness (Kalter, 1998). Other counselors lead same-sex groups in middle school and junior high school to lessen the self-consciousness and decreased self-disclosure that may result from boys and girls in the same group.

**Length and Number of Sessions.** The ideal length of the group sessions also varies according to the age of the children: 20 to 30 minutes is optimal with children 6 years or younger, 30 to 40 minutes is optimal with children between 6 and 9 years old, and 40 to 75 minutes is optimal with children 9 years or older. The number of sessions for a children of divorce group in the schools is typically between 6 and 8. Although it makes sense that a longer group would provide the children with more time to deal with substantive issues, an informal poll of school counselors suggested that because of time constraints, 6 to 8 weekly sessions are all that can be provided within a school year. To counter the limited number of sessions, school counselors reported that students may participate in a children of divorce group during several different grade levels. This format is also useful in that it allows children to address the same issues at different developmental stages and as they encounter issues. It also encourages and supports the idea that it is normal for kids to "repeat" group.

Group length for other settings may vary. Mental health agencies, for example, may be able to sustain longer groups. An ideal length would be 12 to 16 sessions, allowing time to deal with more complex issues such as parental dating and remarriage, communication with new siblings and stepparents, and adaptation to the new family setting. However, court-referred groups most likely will be short-term (e.g., one 4- or 8-hour session or four 2-hour sessions). Because of the length of these workshops and the age of the children involved, it is essential to plan several short activities using a variety of methods to keep the children focused and to keep their involvement and attention levels high. Periodic breaks, usually with some way to channel energy, are also strongly recommended.

**Group Structure.** Structure is essential to providing safety and continuity to the children. Structure is also necessary to manage time efficiently and to focus on relevant issues (DeLucia-Waack, 1996; Gladding, 1991). Depending on the type of group and the age of the children, the level of structure may vary. The younger the children, the more structure is necessary. Psychoeducational groups tend to be more structured, with activities designed to facilitate discussion of a topic and/or development of new skills and behaviors. At the beginning of a session, structure focuses members on what they need to discuss that day, whereas at the end of a session, structure clarifies what has been learned (Gladding, 1991; Morganett, 1990).

Possible ways to begin sessions include check-ins or go-rounds that focus members on what they want to talk about and work on that day, review of homework from previous sessions, or reading a poem or paragraph related to the issues previously discussed in the group. The working part of the session is focused on issues and skill building based on the goals of the group. Teaching and practicing specific skills such as assertiveness, expression of feelings, and communication may be helpful for children of divorce. In addition, techniques such as role-playing and Gestalt empty-chair or two-chair techniques may help children to develop new interpersonal skills and explore issues. Such techniques allow people either to explore and express feelings to other people or to experience two sets of conflicting thoughts and feelings. Some ways to end sessions include summaries (by the leader, by one member, or briefly by all), go-rounds of what each person has learned today and/or thought was most helpful, brief written reactions given to the leader, rating sheets, discussion of homework or things to work on or think about over the next week, or a poem or thought to inspire the week.

Each session outlined later in this manual includes the following components: Review and Check-In or Warm-Up, Working Activities, Processing, and Closing.

**Materials.** Because of the need for creativity in activities with children, it is essential to have a variety of materials on hand. Practical items such as a chalkboard, chalk, paper, crayons, and markers are always needed. In addition, books, videos, and games that focus on divorce are also useful. Furthermore, puppets are especially helpful when working with children in general. It is essential to have a variety of puppets to act out the situations. Group leaders can be creative in their collection of puppets—bath mats, oven mitts, as well as puppets made by the children as an activity all work well. To encourage the expression of a wide range of thoughts, feelings, and verbalizations, it is important to include some puppets that are scary, fuzzy, and furry as well as lots of different roles: queens, kings, princesses, firefighters, police officers, and so forth. Furthermore, an effort should be made to include toys that appeal to a range of ethnic groups.

Each session outlined later in the manual includes at the beginning a list of materials that will be needed for the session. Appendix G lists related materials and resources that may be helpful with children of divorce groups in general.

## STEP 2: RECRUITMENT, SELECTION, SCREENING, AND INFORMED CONSENT OF GROUP MEMBERS

**Recruitment.** Recruitment efforts should focus on children who would like to participate in a children of divorce group and those who are identified by professionals (i.e., counselors, teachers, physicians) and family members as having difficulty adjusting to the divorce. Referrals may come from a variety of sources. In schools, teachers, parents, children, and administrators may all suggest to the counselor that a child may benefit from participation in a children of divorce group. In agencies, referrals may come from counselors who are working with a child in individual counseling as well as from parents and school personnel. Sample recruitment letters to teachers and parents are included in Appendix B. For court-affiliated children of divorce groups, the referral process may be simply that all children under the age of 18 whose parents file for divorce must participate in that district. Thus, it is essential to conduct some kind of initial assessment of what each child's needs are relative to the divorce. This initial assessment is crucial to the selection of appropriate group members for a specific type of group, the development of individual goals for each child, and the assessment of progress throughout the group. Appendix C contains sample instruments and materials.

It is important to keep in mind that although teachers and administrators may be a valuable resource when asking for referrals for a group because they know the children so well, there is also a potential risk of breach of confidentiality. It is helpful to ask teachers to recommend students who may benefit from a children of divorce group because they often know the current family situations of the students and their level of stress related to their family situation. Although a teacher may recommend that a child participate in a children of divorce group and may be helpful in creating time for the child to attend the group, it is important that the teacher understands that the school counselor cannot report back to the teacher about a student's progress in the group and/or disclose what happens in the group. Once a group meeting time has been scheduled, it is important that confidentiality is not violated by, for example, a general announcement that the children of divorce group is meeting now in the library (Ritchie & Huss, 2000). Teachers should be informed that the student is leaving class to meet with the school counselor, but no specifics need be (or should be) given.

**Selection Criteria.** The following general selection criteria are suggested for psychoeducational and counseling groups for children of divorce. First, all children in the group must be within 2 years of each other (Kalter, 1998). Second, siblings should not be in the same group because of conflict of loyalty and the difficulty of the group in acknowledging two perspectives on the same family. Third, ideally there should be a mixture of family situations among the children, with variation in the time since divorce, living situation, parental dating, and remarriage. These differences serve to promote peer role models, generate alternative solutions to problems, and instill hope. Any one child should not be so different in terms of family situation that he or she feels isolated or scapegoated by the group. Although it is impossible to prevent scapegoating, a conscious effort to select and link members on the basis of their similarities (e.g., feelings, experiences) may help group members to make connections and increase cohesiveness among members. It is important that children are able to connect with other children around the issues related to divorce. Each child must have one other child in the group with whom he or she can initially connect and one child who will be able to serve as a role model. In addition, sex and ethnicity of group members should be taken into consideration when trying to prevent scapegoating.

**Screening.** All students should be interviewed by the leader(s) of the group to assess their ability to participate in and benefit from a children of divorce group. An interview, maximum of 30 minutes, should be sufficient to assess (a) the child's willingness to participate, (b) any issues or concerns the child has that are related to the divorce and his or her current living situation, (c) the child's willingness and ability to verbally and nonverbally disclose thoughts and feelings, and (d) the child's ability to follow directions and answer questions asked of him or her. A sample list of interview questions is included in Appendix B. Other potential screening instruments are discussed later in this chapter in the section titled, Step 3: Group Member Needs and Goals Assessment.

**Informed Consent for Parents and Children.** Parental consent is an important issue when working with children of divorce groups. Because of the recent divorce, custody (and who can consent for counseling services) is often an explosive issue for parents. Agency and organization guidelines differ on who can officially provide consent for a minor to receive services. Some agencies require only the custodial parent; others require signatures from both parents if they share joint custody. It is recommended that regardless of the official policy, the leaders of the children of divorce groups make an effort to inform all adults involved with the child, including noncustodial parents, family members with some responsibility for the child, and stepparents, of the goals and focus of the group.

To make an informed decision about participation in a children of divorce group, parents and children must be given information about the type of group; its goals; the format, structure, and typical interventions; and leadership style and credentials of the group leader(s). It is helpful to provide parents with written materials in addition to speaking with them about the group. A one-page handout that summarizes goals, topics, and interventions; discusses the issue of confidentiality; and provides a contact name and phone number is helpful. A sample form for parents is included in Appendix B.

An issue that is often raised when leading children of divorce groups has to do with information and consent needed for a child to participate. It is important to establish with an administrator, whose consent is necessary. Is the consent of the custodial parent alone valid and/or even acceptable when the parents have joint custody? Should the noncustodial parent be informed of the group because it may affect his or her relationship with the child (hopefully positively)? How is consent handled when the child lives with another family member but one or both parents have legal custody? Ritchie and Huss's (2000) article is a valuable reference with regard to how to make decisions related to selection, screening, and recruitment of minors in a way that protects confidentiality and addresses issues of informed consent. They make several valuable suggestions about how to secure parental consent without violating confidentiality. Wilcoxon and Magnusom (1999) also provide specific suggestions about how to balance the needs and demands of custodial and noncustodial parents and, most importantly, the child while taking into consideration each individual situation and ethical and legal issues.

For children, it is important to make sure that they are informed about the group at a level that they can understand. Leaders should choose words that are appropriate to the children's grade level and should use examples whenever possible. It is helpful to explain to children the goals, kinds of activities that may occur in group, and ground rules before they enter the group to ensure that they understand and are ready to participate in group. Appendix B includes a sample informed-consent form that can be read by the children or read to the children depending on their age and reading level.

**Agency or School Consent.** Leaders of a children of divorce group must decide what channels to take to obtain approval to lead the group in their school or agency. Does a proposal need to be submitted? To whom should the proposal be submitted? What should the proposal include? In general, a thorough proposal should include (a) a rationale for the group on the basis of current counseling literature and research and a needs assessment of the population to be served; (b) goals, format, and duration of the group; (c) recruitment, screening, selection, and consent procedures; (d) specific interventions and activities; and (e) evaluation procedures. In a school setting, permission may be needed from any or all of the following people: the head of counseling or guidance services, the principal, the director of pupil services, the superintendent, or the school board. In addition, "acquainting teachers with the effects of family transition on children, information about the group, and the benefits children receive by participating . . . are important" (Beech Acres Aring Institute, 1993, p. 9). In an agency, permission may be needed from the director of clinical services, the director of the agency, and/or the board of directors. Appendix B includes sample forms to inform administrators of the basic goals and structure of this type of children of divorce group.

## STEP 3: GROUP MEMBER NEEDS AND GOALS ASSESSMENT

It is important to collect accurate information about the divorce and the current parental situation from both the child and the parents. Prior to beginning group, it is important to collect the following information from parents: age and sex of all siblings of the child, amount of time since parental separation, current marital status of both parents, custodial situation, and frequency and regularity of visitation with the non-custodial parent. A sample assessment form for parents is included in Appendix C. Children will also provide much of this information from their perspective as they participate in activities in the group. Such activities include describing how they found out about the divorce, drawing pictures of their family and support network, and making a list of reasons why parents get divorced in general, and so forth. A sample list of interview questions for counselors to ask a child to assess appropriateness for group is also included in Appendix B.

Children of divorce often exhibit symptoms of anxiety, depression, and low self-esteem (Spigelman & Spigelman, 1991). Thus, it is important to include measures of anxiety, depression, and self-esteem in an initial assessment. Furthermore, measures designed to assess specific issues of concern related to the divorce for each child are also important. Such measures are important in determining the usefulness of the group intervention and whether additional counseling is needed. Brief descriptions of potential assessment measures are included below. Reliability and validity have been established for each measure. All of the measures described in this section could be given prior to the beginning of a children of divorce group and at the end of the group to assess changes for individual group members as a result of group participation. In addition, measures that assess depression may be used to identify children who may need additional counseling. The measures specific to beliefs and situations related to the divorce may be used to assess commonalities and potential differences between group members.

**Anxiety.** The Revised Children's Manifest Anxiety Scale (Reynolds & Richmond, 1985) consists of 37 statements to which a child responds *yes* or *no*. It measures three factors of anxiety: physiological, worry/oversensitivity, and concentration. It was normed on approximately 5,000 children between 6 and 19 years old, including Caucasian and African American males and females. Sample items include "I have trouble making up my mind," "I am always nice to people," and "I never get angry."

**Depression.** The Children's Depression Inventory (Kovacs, 1981, 1992) is a 27-item symptom inventory that assesses psychomotor, cognitive, and affective dimensions of depression. It was normed on 860 children of divorce. Sample items include "I have fun in many things," "I hate myself," and "I have to push myself many times to do my homework."

**Self-Esteem.** The Perceived Competence Scale for Children (Harter, 1982) consists of 28 items that assess children's perception of competence on physical, cognitive, social, and general self-worth. It was normed on children in Grades 4 to 12. Sample items include "I am good at schoolwork," "I have a lot of friends," "I do well at all sports," and "I am sure of myself."

**Beliefs About Divorce.** The Children's Beliefs About Parental Divorce Scale (Kurdek & Berg, 1987) measures dysfunctional beliefs about divorce and consists of 36 items with six subscales: Peer Ridicule, Avoidance, Paternal Blame, Fear of Abandonment, Hope of Reunification, and Self-Blame. Cronbach's alpha for the entire scale was .79. Additional psychometric information on this scale can be found in Kurdek and Berg's article. The scale is reprinted with permission in Appendix C.

**Group Process.** In addition, it is important to assess what happens in group sessions to further understand the therapeutic factors of groups and, more specifically, how they apply to children's groups and children's methods of learning and integration. To date, no measure of group environment or therapeutic factors has been specifically developed for children or normed on children. Adult measures with some adaptation may be useful but would need to be shortened and/or reworded to a child's reading and comprehension level.

**Critical Incidents in the Group.** The Critical Incidents Questionnaire (Kivlighan & Goldfine, 1991) assesses the most important therapeutic factor for each group member during a specific group session and has been used with minimal rewording with elementary school children (DeLucia-Waack, 2000). After a session, group members can be asked to respond to the following questions either verbally or in writing as an assessment of therapeutic factors: Of all the things that happened in our group today, which was the most helpful for you? Describe what happened and tell why it was important to you. Leaders can then assess what therapeutic factor (Bloch, Reibstein, Crouch, Holroyd, & Themen, 1979; Yalom, 1995) is being described in each answer. Appendix C contains a sample version for children as well as a list of therapeutic factors with which to compare it.

## STEP 4: PLANNING SESSIONS

**Beginning and Ending Sessions.** Regardless of the length of the group, the first session must be devoted to the establishment of ground rules and goals for the group, the introduction of members to each other, and an explanation of the purpose of the group. At the end of the group, at least one session, if not two, must be devoted to termination, with the goals of helping the children (a) summarize what they have learned, (b) express their feelings about the group and the group members, and (c) discuss how they will use what they have learned in their families and outside situations. Termination of the group often brings up abandonment and loss issues for the children related to the divorce and, thus, is often an excellent time to intervene through modeling, expression of feeling, and development of coping plans. In chapter 2, four opening sessions are outlined, whereas chapter 4 includes three termination sessions.

**Choosing the Content of Sessions.** Depending on the individual needs of the children and the number of sessions in the group, the content sessions in the middle of the group might focus on discussion of the family situation (e.g., living arrangements, custody, visitation, extended family, other support); definition of important legal terms (e.g., *separation, divorce, custody, courts*) and information about divorce; identification and evaluation of worries and beliefs, specifically magical thinking and irrational beliefs about the divorce (e.g., "I'll never see my father again," "I can get my parents back together again," "We'll be homeless," "My Dad left me so my Mom may leave me too," "It is my fault that they got divorced"); expression of feelings about the divorce (e.g., anger, sadness, grief, loneliness, relief); solutions to problems generated by problem-solving around difficult situations (e.g., visitation, new parental relationships, parental fighting, parental dating, blended families, stepparents, stepsiblings); and development of skills to deal with difficult situations (e.g., communication, conflict resolution, anger management, expression of feelings).

**Initial Assessment of Important Issues Related to Divorce.** Group facilitators of the Boys and Girls Groups (Beech Acres Aring Institute, 1993) use a checklist that directly asks children what issues related to the divorce are affecting them. The checklist is completed prior to the group or during the first two sessions. After each child in a specific group has completed the checklist, the compilation of answers is used to choose the focus of psychoeducational sessions. There are three versions that are based on children's grade level: Grades 1–3, 4–6, and 7–12. The topic areas include the divorce experience, parental fighting, legal aspects of the divorce, feelings of being caught in the middle, how to maintain parental relationships, changes since the divorce, parents' new partners, stepfamilies, traditions and holidays, and future family plans. The Beech Acres' form is reprinted with permission in Appendix C.

## STEP 5: LEADER PREPARATION FOR GROUP

**Coleadership.** Coleadership for a children of divorce group is preferable, specifically a male–female coleadership team (DeLucia-Waack, 1996). The benefits of coleadership are helpful in any group: two role models, two leaders who can cooperate and work together, and two sets of eyes and ears to observe the content and process of the group. In addition, for children of divorce groups, a male–female coleadership team can model collaboration between male and female adults and can provide contact with supportive and caring adults of both sexes. A male presence in the group is particularly important because many of the children may not have much contact with a male adult, especially if they are in an elementary school setting (Kalter, 1998). Although such a model of coleadership may be time-intensive and difficult to arrange, it is highly valuable and worth the effort. The coleader does not necessarily need to be a counselor. If the group is psychoeducational in nature and, thus, is fairly structured in its content, it is necessary to have only one counselor as a leader. The other leader could be a teacher if the groups are led in school. However, it is important that the second coleader is able to be empathic and supportive and to provide some structure to the group. In agencies, it may be possible to recruit a youth worker or a caseworker who works with children but who hasn't been trained as a counselor. Another combination that has worked in elementary schools but could be used in agencies as well is to have a high school student who has experienced a parental divorce. This person can be supportive and may also be able to share how he or she felt when this happened to him or her. In addition, the children may be able to connect more easily with an older student.

Regardless of coleaders' skills and experience, they must commit to weekly planning and supervision sessions to prepare for their group and to process what has happened. A dedicated hour each week is essential to working cooperatively with a coleader. The time is spent planning individual goals and strategies for each child, reviewing session events and group process, and planning for future sessions. When coleadership is not possible, a group counselor leading a group by himself or herself should still set aside an hour a week to plan and process for the group.

**Preparation for Group Leaders.** To prepare for the group, counselors need to think about it from several different perspectives. How will they as counselors personally and professionally prepare for the group? How will they prepare others for the group, specifically their school or agency (including administrators), parents, and children? As counselors begin to get ready for a children of divorce group, they need to have a sense of their beliefs about divorce, the needs of children of divorce, and how a group can best help these children. To do this, they first must examine their own personal values and experiences with divorce and separation. Second, they must examine the current counseling literature about what is most effective with children of divorce in terms of themes, interventions, structure, and so forth. See Appendix G for a list of suggested readings for counselors. To begin to establish trust and cooperation with their coleader, they should meet regularly before the group starts to discuss theoretical orientation, leadership style, and goals and interventions for the group. Each coleader should assess his or her strengths and weaknesses as a leader of the particular children of divorce group that he or she is planning. Assessment of the group leadership skills needed for this group should include the type of group (psychoeducational or counseling), the age of the children, and the focus and goals of the group. The Co-Facilitating Inventory (Pfeiffer & Jones, 1975) is a good resource for leaders to examine their own style of leadership individually and provides a structured format for discussions between coleaders.

*Chapter*

# 2

# Introductory Sessions

- **Introduce children to each other.**
- **Introduce children to the purpose and structure of the group.**
- **Identify individual and group goals.**
- **Reduce initial anxiety.**

The goals of the first session(s) of psychoeducational groups generally focus on the following: introducing the children to the goals, content, organization, and structure of the group; introducing the children to each other; helping them to think about why they are in this particular group; and helping them to deal with their anxiety about being in the group and about the topic. For children of divorce groups specifically, the first few sessions are organized around getting the children to know each other and the focus of the group. It is recommended that at least 2 sessions be introductory sessions, though with a shorter group (fewer than 8 sessions), 1 session may be all that can be allotted. If that is the case, Session I-A is recommended. For groups of 8 to 16 sessions in length, Sessions I-A and I-B are recommended. For longer groups or ones that need to build cohesiveness because of a great deal of member mistrust or resistance, Sessions I-A, I-B, and I-C are suggested.

Even though in a school setting children may often know each other, it is still important to spend some time having children introduce themselves and say something about themselves that casual contact in school would not provide. An initial icebreaker should include each child's name, to make sure that everyone knows everyone else (and how to correctly pronounce their names), and some kind of self-disclosure. The self-disclosure may be rather superficial (e.g., something that makes me happy . . . ), but it establishes a norm: that we self-disclose about ourselves and our feelings.

Once children have introduced themselves, it is important to talk about how the group works and what will make this group safe. A quick discussion of topics and the role of the leader should be followed by a more detailed discussion of ground rules, including confidentiality and how interaction will occur (only respectful comments, only one person talks at a time, etc.). Children should be informed in the first session, if not before, when the group will meet, for how long, and where. Specifics such as how they will get to the group (e.g., a pass will be sent, a teacher will bring them, the school counselor will pick them up) should also be discussed.

Initial sessions should also include a discussion of the general goals of the group, followed by a discussion of individual goals for each child. Even young children can understand and participate in such discussions. They need to know that they will be focusing on identifying and disclosing feelings and thoughts related to their divorce situation and what potential topics may be focused on. They can also identify specific issues for them (either on their own or through pregroup screening, assessment, and interviews) that they would like to work on or change during the course of the group. Typical goals include "I don't want to feel so caught in the middle between my Mom and Dad," "I don't want to feel guilty when I am with one parent," and "I want to feel less sad when I think about my parents splitting up."

Providing specific information about what will happen in the group sessions and about the role of the leader will help to reduce children's anxiety. Their anxiety will also be reduced by participating in the screening interviews with the group leader. In the first session, disclosing about the divorce and finding that others have similar situations is particularly helpful in alleviating initial anxiety related to group participation.

Three opening sessions follow.

# Session Topics

| MAJOR TOPIC | SESSION TOPIC | SESSION NUMBER |
|---|---|---|
| *Introduction* | Introduction to Each Other and to the Group | I-A |
| | Lots of Children Have Parents Who Are Divorced | I-B |
| | How Our Group Can Work Together | I-C |
| *Divorce Experience* | How Divorce Happened in My Family | 1-A |
| | What Are Our Families Like? | 1-B |
| | Our Families and Friends: Who Can We Talk To? | 1-C |
| | Worries | 1-D |
| | Worries About the Divorce and Who Is Responsible for Them | 1-E |
| | Is It My Fault? | 1-F |
| *Feelings* | Feelings About the Divorce | 2-A |
| | The Emotional Process of Divorce | 2-B |
| | Sad Feelings About the Divorce or Separation | 2-C |
| | Feeling Angry About the Divorce | 2-D |
| *Communication Skills* | Communication Skills | 3-A |
| | Nonverbal Communication | 3-B |
| *Parental Fighting* | How to Cope With Parental Fighting | 4 |
| *Legal Aspects* | What Do All the Big Words Mean for Me? | 5-A |
| | Visitation | 5-B |
| *Caught in the Middle* | Some Ways to Cope With Parents Who Don't Live Together | 6 |

| MAJOR TOPIC | SESSION TOPIC | SESSION NUMBER |
|---|---|---|
| *Maintaining Parental Relationships* | Maintaining Parental Relationships | 7 |
| *Changes* | Life Is Tough and Some Ways to Cope With It | 8-A |
| | Different Types of Families | 8-B |
| | New Traditions | 8-C |
| *Parents' New Partners* | I Tried to Get My Mom and Dad Back Together Again | 9-A |
| | Still Trying to Get My Mom and Dad Back Together Again | 9-B |
| | New People in Our Lives | 9-C |
| | My Mom and Dad Are Dating Other People? | 9-D |
| *Stepfamilies* | Coping With Blended Families | 10-A |
| | The Stages of Stepfamilies | 10-B |
| *Ending* | Ending | E-A |
| | What Have I Learned From This Group? | E-B |
| | What Can I Do Differently? | E-C |

# I-A

# Introduction to Each Other and to the Group

## GROUP SESSION

As children are entering the room, play the song **"Divorce"** in the background. Ask the children to sit in a circle.

*Icebreaker* (10 minutes)

1. **Introductory Exercise to Remember Names** (8 minutes). Welcome to our group. We are going to do an exercise to learn names and a little bit about each person. Everyone will state *My name is . . . and one thing I like to do that makes me happy is . . . .* As the group leader and model for the group, you begin by telling your name and one activity that you like to do. Then ask who wants to go next. Tell them that they must first tell your name and what you like to do, then their own name and what they like to do. Each child repeats all the children's names before him or her and what they like to do. They can ask each other for help if they forget a name or an activity.

   After each child has spoken, then ask the children if they have questions for each other or something that they want to say—such as "I like to do that, too. And here's why" or "How did you learn to do that?" Go on when no one has another comment or each child has made a comment/question and has been acknowledged by the child they spoke to. Encourage the children to speak directly to each other and answer the person who has spoken.

2. **Group Rules** (2 minutes). End with the statement that this is one of the first rules in group—that when

we want to tell someone something, we look at them and say it directly to them. Before we can actually start working together as a group there are some things we need to decide to get our group going. First, we need to decide on rules for our group so that everyone feels safe and wants to talk and share in the group. Write this ground rule on the large notepad under the heading Group Rules.

*Working Activities* (27 minutes)

3. **Agreement on Group Norms and Rules** (10 minutes). We need group rules to start. Ask the children to come up with a list of ground rules to make the group safe. Give examples of each (or ask them to explain what they think the rule means and then give examples). Also explain why each rule helps make the group a safe place and also ensures that each child gets to talk. Write (or have a child write) the ground rules on the large notepad as they are discussed.

   **Possible Ground Rules:**
   Everyone gets a chance to talk.
   One person speaks at a time.
   No hitting or fighting in group.

4. **Discussion of Confidentiality and What It Means** (2 minutes). Also, talk about when you as a leader might need to break confidentiality. For example, you might say: Confidentiality for our group means that whatever everyone says in group stays here. We don't talk about what happens in group outside of the group time we have set aside each week. If you want to talk about what you did or said in group or your feelings about group, you may tell others. You can always talk to me and the school counselor(s) about what happens in group. To your friends and your family, you cannot talk about what other people have said. Also, please don't talk to someone else in the group about group because people not in the group might hear. Don't talk about group on the playground or in class. That would break confidentiality. There are a few times when I would have to talk about things one of you said in group—if someone talks about harming themselves or others, if someone talks about child abuse, or if a judge in a court of law asks me. Otherwise, specific things that other people say stay in this room until the next time we meet and can talk about them. Add confidentiality as a ground rule.

5. **Clarification of Confidentiality** (5 minutes). Have each child state: *One thing that I can say out of group is XXX, and one thing that I could say that would break confidentiality is XXX.* Start with yourself saying: One thing I could say out of group is that I felt both happy and sad this week in group, but I can't say that Suzie was happy and sad. Gently correct them if needed by rephrasing and changing a word or two.

6. **Introduce Music to the Group** (8 minutes). We are going to use music to help us talk about what is happening in our lives, specifically around the divorce or

separation of our parents. Play the **"Divorce"** song. Ask the children to listen to the song for the main points of the song. Encourage them to sing along and to move to the music. When the song ends, have them sit down. Then ask them to identify the major themes of the song. Write them on the large notepad.

**Potential Themes:**
Mom and Dad didn't get along so they got divorced
Things don't always go right or the way we want them to
Divorce hurts
Divorce happens to lots of children
Sometimes you feel anger and sadness
When you talk about the divorce and all of the feelings, it doesn't hurt so bad
Everyone thinks marriage is forever
Divorce is hard on the children, too

7. **Explain the Purpose and Goals of the Group** (2 minutes). This group will focus on helping you cope with the divorce or separation and all the new feelings and things that happen to you as your family changes and adjusts to the divorce or separation. We will use songs to focus on different topics and then to help you learn new ways to cope. What will be fun about this group is that we will be using music to do this. Dan Conley wrote and sang these songs for his children when he was going through a divorce. Kelly and Cory also sing the songs and offer some thoughts about divorce from a kid's perspective. Did you hear Kelly and Cory singing? Dan is the father so he sings the main part, then Kelly comes in . . . , and then Cory comes in . . . . (As you talk, underline the related themes on the large notepad: divorce hurts; divorce happens to lots of children; sometimes you feel anger and sadness; when you talk about it, it feels better; and divorce is hard on the children, too.)

*Processing* (6 minutes)

8. Being a child of divorce is hard at times. There are a lot of different issues that need to be addressed. Let's everyone go around and finish the sentence: *The most important issue for children of divorce is XXX.*

*Closing* (2 minutes)

9. Hand out **"If You Believe in You"** tapes and ask the children to listen to **"Divorce"** during the week. Tell them that listening to music helps them to calm down and feel better sometimes. We want them to listen to the tape to help them feel better.

*Homework*

10. Think about a name for our group. We'll decide next week.

# I-B

# Lots of Children Have Parents Who Are Divorced

## GROUP SESSION

*Review* (13 minutes)

1. Sing the **"Divorce"** song (3 minutes).

2. **Review of Names** (4 minutes). Everyone says the name of the person sitting to their right. They can ask for help if they need to.

3. **Review of Group Rules** (6 minutes). Write them on a large piece of material or heavy paper in the center, leaving space at the top for the name of the group and around the sides for the members to personalize their banner. This banner will be hung during each group session. As a child says a ground rule, write it on the banner.

*Working Activities* (25 minutes)

4. **Choose a Group Name** (15 minutes). This is our group to help us deal with our feelings, thoughts, and situations related to our parents' separation or divorce. We have ground rules and goals; now we need a name. What shall we call ourselves? Have each child state at least one name for the group and why they think that is a name that reflects their group and its goals. Then discuss which name they like. If necessary, have them vote on a name. Add the name to the banner and then have everyone add a sign or symbol for themselves.

5. **Whose Parents Are Divorced or Separated?** (10 minutes). There are a lot of parents who get divorced or who separate, which leaves lots of children like you. The song **"Divorce"** says that Ashley's and Sue's and Jaime's and Amy's and Andy's parents all got divorced. Let's make a list of children we know whose parents don't live together. Let's start with Kelly and Cory. Then us. Who else? Any celebrities? Any adults?

   Make a list on poster board.

*Processing* (4 minutes)

6. There are a lot of people in this world whose parents get divorced. In fact, just about every other person is a child of divorce. So now that we know this, let's everyone go around and finish the sentence: *Now that I know other kids whose parents are divorced or separated, I . . . .*

*Closing* (3 minutes)

7. Sing the **"Divorce"** song.

*Homework*

8. Ask the children to listen to the **"Divorce"** song during the week when they think about the divorce.

# I-C

# How Our Group Can Work Together

## GROUP SESSION

*Review* (8 minutes)

1. Play and sing the **"Divorce"** song (3 minutes).

2. **Review of Group Name and Group Rules** (5 minutes). Let's just remind ourselves one more time who we are as a group and how we will make this group safe. Here's our banner hanging on the wall so we always know who we are and what our rules are.

*Working Activities* (30 minutes)

3. **What Should This Group Talk About?** (10 minutes). Now that we have a name for our group and we know how we will make this group safe, let's decide what it is OK to talk about.

4. In the **"Divorce"** song, Dan suggests a lot of things that children might want to talk about in this group, such as how you found out about divorce; your feelings: angry, sad, scared, or sometimes relieved; what if your parents date or marry someone else; what about new sisters or brothers; and how you talk to parents and talk about your feelings. What else can we talk about in this group? This group is a special place because all of you have had something similar happen to you and so it is a little easier to talk about and be understood. What do you think we should talk about in this group? Let's make a list. If they are quiet, you can prompt them with: What do you think Kelly

20

and Cory might want to talk about? Or what do you think children of divorce need to talk about?

That's a great list. Let's keep it to remind ourselves of what we should be talking about in here.

5. **How Should This Group Work?** (20 minutes). Hand out four small pieces of paper to each member. Now that we have this great list of what children of divorce should talk about in their group, let's decide how to make this group work for each one of you. Let's talk briefly about how this group has been helpful for each of you so far. We will all write down some things about the group, and then I'll read them out loud without saying who wrote them. Let's each write down on a piece of paper one thing that you have learned in this group so far.

One thing that happened in group that made you feel better . . .

One person in group who has helped you and how . . .

One thing that you want to talk about in this group is . . .

Have the children fold up the papers as they write them, collect the papers after each question, and then mix them up before reading them. You can read the answers after each question or after all of them.

*Processing* (4 minutes)

6. **Connections.** Many of you were probably feeling or thinking what others wrote. Let's make sure that others know that we have similar thoughts or feelings. Let's everyone go around and finish the sentence: *I feel close to the person who wrote XXX* (XXX should be something that was written on a piece of paper).

*Closing* (3 minutes)

7. Listen to (and sing along if you like) **"Everybody Needs A Friend."**

*Homework*

8. Ask the children to listen to **"Everybody Needs A Friend"** during the week when they need a friend.

# 3

# Content Sessions

- Each session includes a Review or Warm-Up, Working Activities, Processing, and Closing.
- Nonverbal techniques are included as interventions to help the children identify and discuss important feelings and issues.
- Universalizing statements are included throughout the sessions to normalize experiences and provide information.
- Each session includes at least one song.
- Content sessions are arranged by topic and sequentially.

The sessions that follow in this chapter are the middle sessions, or the content sessions, of the group. In chapter 2, the introductory sessions were discussed and provided for your use. Chapter 4 discusses and includes possible ending sessions.

There is a format for each session because children need a great deal of structure in their groups. Each content session includes a Review or Warm-Up that connects to material in a previous session and/or introduces the topic for this session (typically 5 to 8 minutes), Working Activities that allow the children to discuss and interact around a specific topic (typically 25 to 30 minutes), Processing that typically includes questions to help make sense of the Working Activities (typically 4 to 5 minutes), and a Closing that helps relax the children and prepare them to leave group (usually a song; typically 3 to 5 minutes). Sessions are written to aid the counselors leading them, with suggested dialogue being provided whenever possible.

In addition, children usually respond better to nonverbal techniques than to verbal exercises because of their limited vocabularies and their dispositions to display feelings through play (Gladding, 1991). Thus, puppets, role-plays, the writing of songs and plays, and projection of thoughts and feelings onto Kelly and Cory (and Dan, Phyllis, and Jean) are commonly used techniques. Two techniques common in counseling work with children, displacement activities and universalizing statements (Kalter, 1998), are used throughout the sessions. Displacement activities include playing with puppets, using dolls and action figures, and talking about fictional and real characters (e.g., Dan, Kelly, Cory, and Jean). The safety of the "one step removed" technique allows the children to talk about their feelings while cloaked in the displacement activities. A child may not be able to answer the question "How did it feel when your parents told you they were getting a divorce?" but he or she may be able to answer the question "How do you think Kelly and Cory felt when they found out their parents were getting a divorce?"

Universalizing statements are used by group counselors to discuss important divorce-related topics and events without specifically addressing one group member. They allow the group counselor to provide important information about typical reactions, questions, and concerns related to the divorce, such as "children of divorce often are worried that their mother (whichever parent has custody) will leave them, too" or "children of divorce often worry that they are the reason why their parents got divorced." A universalizing statement with the goal of normalizing the situations and feelings related to divorce or of providing information to the children is included at the beginning of each processing activity.

Yauman (1991) suggested that bibliotherapy, the use of books and films in therapy, has been particularly effective in helping children of divorce express their feelings about the divorce. Children deal with their feelings indirectly through the use of books and films. In early sessions of group work, books and videos can be used as stimuli that the children can view, listen to, and then reflect on. For example, after reading a book about a family whose parents got divorced, the group leader might begin the discussion with the following questions: How did the children in the book feel? How did they express their feelings? Behaviorally? Verbally? Nonverbally? In later sessions, children may be encouraged to write their own books about divorce that describe what happens for children. They can show how children can deal with divorce as a way of expressing their feelings and then actively prescribing ways to cope with the feelings and the situation surrounding the divorce. See Appendix G for potential books and videos.

Because young children are often unable to express their feelings, thoughts, and potential fears, the use of play in groups is also beneficial. Used along with songs and bibliotherapy, puppets help take the information and situations in the songs and books and make them real for children. After listening to a song or reading a book, the group leader can say to the children: "Let's act out the story now." For instance, in one of the early sessions of a children of divorce group, the children may listen to a song or read a book about how children find out that their parents are getting a divorce. The children may then act out the situation, with each child choosing a puppet to portray a specific person: mother, father, children, and/or important figures in the situation. The group leader can act as a facilitator of the puppet show, instructing the parents to disclose certain information to the children (e.g., reasons for the divorce, they will still see them every week), the children to express feelings or ask certain questions to the parents, or to back up and replay a situation in a different way (e.g., now react with anger or sadness instead of saying that everything is OK).

Dan Conley's songs are interspersed throughout most sessions. The songs are used to introduce a topic, begin discussion, lead to an activity, end a session with positive affect, suggest coping strategies outside of group, serve as a coping strategy outside of group, and channel energy. Each session uses at least one song; many sessions use two or three songs. For example, **"Divorce"** is often used as an introduction to a topic or can be used to channel energy. **"So Am I"** and **"If You Believe In You"** are often used to end sessions with positive affect. **"Everybody Needs A Friend"** is used to suggest coping strategies outside of group as well as to serve as a coping strategy.

The 26 content sessions are arranged by topic and sequentially. After the important issues for each specific group have been identified—by interview, an informal assessment, or a formal assessment such as the one in Appendix C—then important topics to cover and specific sessions can be identified. Topics are arranged to flow between and within topics. It is recommended that sessions be presented in sequence. For example, Session 8 should not be used before Session 4. Each session can be used independently, or the sessions can be used sequentially to build on discussion and learning from the previous session on the same topic. For example, there are several sessions on parents' new partners. If that is an important topic for a children of divorce group to discuss on the basis of the members' needs, then one session might be enough and any of Session 9 (A, B, C, or D) could be used. If it is a topic that many of the children report needing to spend time on, several sessions might be devoted to that topic, in which case the sessions should be ordered as they follow each other in the chapter. Following is a list of the topics covered in sessions and the titles of those sessions. The Initial Assessment in Appendix C is useful in determining what sessions a specific group (or group member) might benefit from.

# 1-A

# How Divorce Happened in My Family

## GOALS FOR THE SESSION

1. To define divorce and separation.
2. To discuss the current situations of each child in the group.
3. To explore the feelings associated with divorce.
4. To introduce the "So Am I" song as a way to cope.

## MATERIALS

- Banner with group name and ground rules hanging on the wall
- "If You Believe In You" tape (specifically the "Divorce" and "So Am I" songs)
- Large notepad and markers
- Words to the "Divorce" song

## GROUP SESSION

*Review and Check-In* (8 minutes)

1. Sing the **"Divorce"** song (3 minutes).

2. **Check-In** (5 minutes). Let's see how everyone is doing today. Let's go around in a circle and everyone state *One time that I listened to the* **"Divorce"** *song this week was XXX because XXX.* If they didn't listen to the song, have them state when they might have wanted to.

*Working Activities* (25 minutes)

3. **Finding Out About the Divorce** (2 minutes). Let's think about the **"Divorce"** song for a minute. How did Dan find out that his parents were getting divorced? His parents separated and told him that they were getting divorced at the same time. His parents sat him down on a rainy day in the morning and said they had something serious to say. Does everyone know the difference between separated and divorced? Separation means that a husband and wife are not going to live together anymore and they may be thinking about a divorce. Divorce means that a husband and wife are no longer married but they are still parents to the children from the marriage. A court of law makes it official that they are no longer married.

4. **How Did Your Parents Tell You?** (12 minutes). Let's talk about how you found out that your parents were getting divorced or separated. Let each child tell what happened to them.

5. How did Cory in the **"Divorce"** song feel about the divorce? What did he say? Cory was shocked . . . he could not believe . . . that one was going to stay and the other was going to leave . . . (1 minute).

6. **Identification of Feelings About Divorce** (10 minutes). Let's talk about all the feelings that Kelly and Cory felt about the divorce. Let's look at a feeling chart (or list of feeling words) and circle all the feelings that they might have had. Now let's talk about why they had each feeling.

*Processing* (5 minutes)

7. Sometimes it is hard to talk about the divorce. But it helps when you have others to talk to because you find out who is having the same problems and the same feelings. Let's everyone go around and finish the sentence: *One person I think has the same feelings or same thing happen to them is XXX.*

*Closing* (7 minutes)

8. Music makes people feel good when they sing. Let's sing a new song today that will maybe make you feel a little better when you are sad. Let's listen to it once and then sing the chorus. You'll catch on quickly.

9. Play **"So Am I."**

10. Get in a circle, hold hands, and play **"So Am I."** Sing the chorus.

> **Life is tough**
> **So am I**
> **So am I**
> **So am I**

*Homework*

11. Ask the children to listen to **"So Am I"** when life gets tough during the week.

# 1-B

# What Are Our Families Like?

## GROUP SESSION

*Review and Check-In* (7 minutes)

1. Sing the **"So Am I"** song (3 minutes).

2. **Check-In** (4 minutes). Let's see how everyone is doing today. Did anyone listen to **"So Am I"** this week? When? Let's go around and say *I was tough this week when XXX happened to me.*

*Working Activities* (30 minutes)

3. **What Do Our Families Look Like?** (10 minutes). Today our topic is families. Everyone's family is a little different, and you all are here in this group because your parents are divorced, separated, or don't live together. We are going to start first with who lives in your house. Let the children draw for about 8 minutes—encourage them to draw an outline of a house in the center of the paper and then draw everyone who lives in the house with them. Circulate as they draw and answer questions as needed.

4. **Who Lives With Us?** (10 minutes). Have each child tell who lives in their house and a little bit about each person—what they like to do, what the child likes to do with them, how well do they get along. As you talk, explain that each family is a little different, but we will also see similarities, too. Some people live with their mother; some live with their father. Sometimes mothers and fathers don't get

married or live together at all so a child always lives with one parent. Sometimes they live with grandparents or aunts or uncles, too.

5. **Who Doesn't Live With Us But Is Part of Our Family?** (10 minutes). Now let's look at who else is in your family. Who doesn't live in your house but is related to you, like mothers, fathers, brothers, sisters, stepmothers, and stepfathers? Let's draw the rest of your family around your house. Let them draw for about 8 minutes. Circulate as they draw and answer questions as needed.

6. Let's save these pictures because next week we'll talk about our families some more.

7. Collect the drawings for the next session.

*Processing* (5 minutes)

8. **Connections.** It is nice to know that some people have families that are similar to ours. It is also helpful in this group to have some differences, too, so that we sometimes will have different ideas to share. Let's everyone go around and finish the sentence: *I like it that XXX is like me in XXX way.*

*Closing* (3 minutes)

9. Sing the **"So Am I"** song.

*Homework*

10. Ask the children to listen to **"So Am I"** when life gets tough during the week.

# 1-C

# Our Families and Friends: Who Can We Talk To?

## GROUP SESSION

*Check-In* (5 minutes)

1. **Check-In.** Look at the feeling chart and state *I felt XXX and so I listened to XXX song.* If they didn't listen to a song, what did they do?

*Working Activities* (32 minutes)

2. Pass out the drawings of families from last week.

3. **Who Is Part of Our Family But Doesn't Live With Us?** (8 minutes). Ask everyone to look at their drawings of who is in their family but doesn't live with them. Have them tell about each of their family members—what they like to do, what the child likes to do with them, and how well they get along.

4. **What Makes a Friend?** (3 minutes). We all have families, but we all also have friends and other people like teachers, neighbors, and school counselors who support us and listen to us. Let's listen to a song about sometimes needing to talk to other people about "stuff." It is called **"Everybody Needs A Friend."** As we listen, think about what makes a friend? Play **"Everybody Needs A Friend."**

5. **Our Friends** (7 minutes). Now let's draw some more people—your friends and other people who love and support you now and whom you can talk to.

6. Tell who each person is and why it feels good to be with that person (7 minutes).

7. **Talking to Someone Is Helpful** (4 minutes). Sometimes it helps to talk about things that make you mad or sad or even about things that are good. Why does it help to talk to someone? Make a list on a large notepad of why it is good to talk to people about the divorce or separation.

8. Let's go back through all three of our pictures and circle everyone whom we can talk to when we are feeling down (3 minutes).

*Processing* (5 minutes)

9. It is nice to know that there are people, adults and children, whom we can talk to about our feelings. Let's everyone go around and finish the sentence: *One person I can talk to about the divorce is XXX.*

*Closing* (3 minutes)

10. Sing **"Everybody Needs A Friend."**

*Homework*

11. Ask the children to listen to **"Everybody Needs A Friend"** when they feel down this week and then talk to someone.

# 1-D

# Worries

## Goals for the Session

1. To explore worries about the divorce.
2. To identify ways to deal with worries.
3. To identify whose job it is to worry about specific things: parents or children.
4. To identify ways to cope with worries.

## Materials

- Banner with group name and ground rules hanging on the wall
- **"If You Believe In You"** tape (specifically "Everybody Needs A Friend" and "I Worry" songs)
- Large notepad and markers
- A variety of puppets
- Words to "Everybody Needs A Friend" song

## GROUP SESSION

*Check-In* (8 minutes)

1. Play **"Everybody Needs A Friend"** (3 minutes).

2. **Everybody Needs a Friend to Talk To** (5 minutes). Have everyone go around and state *I talked to my friend named XXX this week about this problem XXX.*

*Working Activities* (29 minutes)

3. Today we are going to talk about fears that children may have about divorce. Let's listen to this song called **"I Worry"** and then talk about it.

4. Play **"I Worry"** (3 minutes).

5. **What Do Kids Worry About?** (3 minutes). This is Kelly singing about what she is worried about since the divorce. Who is she worried about? Her brother, mother, father, and Kelly. What is she worried about? Who's happy and who's sad? Who will be there when she is sad, has a problem, cries? And also when she smiles and has ice cream?

6. **What Else Do Kids Worry About?** (8 minutes). Ask what else kids worry about. Write all the worries down on a large notepad. Label the left-hand column: "Worries." Leave some space to the right of each worry to fill in later.

7. **Whose Worry Is It?** (8 minutes). Now label the right-hand column on the large notepad: "Whose

worry?" Tell the children that sometimes there are things that they need to worry about and sometimes there are things that only adults need to worry about. Suggest that it is helpful that we figure out whose worries are whose so we don't worry about things that we can't control or shouldn't have to worry about. Suggest that it might be helpful to come up with a phrase to help us remember whose worries are whose, such as BP for big people's worries or MD for Mom and Dad's worries. Let them brainstorm for a minute. Then go through the list that they have generated and have them decide for each worry whether they should worry about it or whether it is a big people's worry.

8. **What Can We Do About Our Worries?** (7 minutes). Now let's make a list of what we can do about our worries. What kinds of things make us feel good? Or help us to problem solve about our worries?

*Processing* (5 minutes)

9. Everyone worries. But what is most important is to decide which things to worry about and which things to let go. Let's everyone go around and finish the sentence: *One thing that kids worry about is XXX, and they can do XXX to feel better.*

*Closing* (3 minutes)

10. Sing **"Everybody Needs A Friend."**

*Homework*

11. Ask the children to listen to one of the songs when they feel down this week.

# 1-E

# Worries About the Divorce and Who Is Responsible for Them

**GOALS FOR THE SESSION**

1. To identify specific worries that group members may have as a result of the divorce.
2. To practice talking with parents about worries.

**MATERIALS**

- Banner with group name and ground rules hanging on the wall
- "If You Believe In You" tape (specifically "Everybody Needs A Friend," "I Worry," and "So Am I" songs)
- Large notepad and markers
- List of worries from Session 1-D
- Puppets for 2 parents and 2 children

## GROUP SESSION

*Review* (10 minutes)

1. Play **"Everybody Needs A Friend"** (3 minutes).

2. **Whom Can I Talk To in This Group?** (7 minutes). Have everyone go around and state: *If I need to talk, I can talk to XXX (someone in this group) about the divorce because I know that they will listen to me. Thank you.*

*Working Activities* (28 minutes)

3. I am going to play the song **"I Worry."** Kelly is singing about what and whom she worries about. We listened to it before and then made a list of worries.

4. Play **"I Worry"** (3 minutes).

5. **Worries List** (3 minutes). Sometimes children do worry about stuff even though last time we decided that parents, or big people, should worry about it. Let's take out our list and talk about it again. Any worries that should be added to the list?

6. **Guidelines for Parents** (8 minutes). Sometimes it helps to talk to our parents about our worries. We are going to use puppets to do this, but before we do, let's talk about how we want our parents to respond to us when we talk to them about our worries. Ask them to come up with some guidelines about how they want the parent puppet to respond.

7. **Puppet Role-Play of How to Talk to Parents** (14 minutes). Let's use puppets to do this. Let's have some kids talk with their parents about what they are worried about. Let's look at our list of what kids worry about.

   A. **Kelly talking to her father, Dan** (4 minutes). Let's have Kelly talk to Dan first about one of her worries. Ask someone to be Dan; ask someone to be Kelly (choose puppets ahead of time). Assign the worry by whispering it in Kelly's ear.

   B. **Cory talking to his mother, Jean** (4 minutes). Let's have Cory talk to Jean about one of his worries. Ask someone to be Jean; ask someone to be Cory (choose puppets ahead of time). Assign the worry by whispering it in Cory's ear.

   C. **Kelly talking to her mother, Jean** (3 minutes). Let's have Kelly talk to Jean about one of her worries. Ask someone to be Jean; ask someone to be Kelly (choose puppets ahead of time). Assign the worry by whispering it in Kelly's ear.

   D. **Cory talking to his father, Dan** (3 minutes). Let's have Cory talk to Dan about one of his worries. Ask someone to be Dan; ask someone to be Cory (choose puppets ahead of time). Assign the worry by whispering it in Cory's ear.

   Group leader should serve as the coach for the mother or father, suggesting or reframing comments as necessary to help the parent to be supportive and helpful.

*Processing* (4 minutes)

8. It is very helpful to be able to talk to your parents about your worries. Grown-ups often say things that help children to feel better. Let's everyone go around and finish the sentence: *I liked when XXX (the mother or father) said XXX because XXX (Kelly or Cory) then felt better.*

*Closing* (3 minutes)

9. Sing **"So Am I."**

*Session*

# 1-F

# Is It My Fault?

## Goals for the Session

1. To explore fears and anxieties about the divorce.
2. To explore the belief that the divorce is the child's fault.
3. To dispute the belief that the child caused the divorce.
4. To discuss ways to ask parents about this and other fears.

## Materials

- Banner with group name and ground rules hanging on the wall
- "If You Believe In You" tape (specifically "And I Need A Lot Of Love" and "Is It My Fault?" songs)
- Large notepad and markers
- Words to "And I Need A Lot Of Love" and "Is It My Fault?" songs

## GROUP SESSION

*Check-In* (8 minutes)

1. Let's sing **"And I Need A Lot Of Love"** (3 minutes).

2. **Check-In** (5 minutes). Ask them to state: *I listened to XXX song this week because . . . .*

*Working Activities* (29 minutes)

3. Let's listen to another song. It's called **"Is It My Fault?"**

4. Play **"Is It My Fault?"** (3 minutes).

5. That is Cory singing. He is Dan's son, and he was 3 years old when Dan and his mother separated. What is Cory afraid of? What makes him think that he caused the divorce? His room is a mess; he doesn't always do his best (2 minutes).

6. **Is It My Fault?** (8 minutes). Why would children like Cory think that it is their fault? Make a list.

7. What does Dan say about divorce? That it is never the kid's fault. He tells Cory that it is not his fault. It is never due to what the kid did.

8. **Why Do People Get Divorced?** (5 minutes). Let's talk about reasons why people get divorced. What did your parents tell you? Let's make a list of why

36

people get divorced. Parents get divorced because they don't love each other anymore. Sometimes they can't live together without fighting and making the other person sad, so they decide to live apart. They have different ways of doing things, and they can't work together as a couple. They love someone else.

9. Do any of you think it is your fault? What do other children think about this on the basis of what we have talked about? (5 minutes).

10. **It's Not Your Fault** (3 minutes). Let's sing **"Is It My Fault?"** Let's stand in a circle and help Cory know that it's not his fault. Let's sing the part of Cory's parents.

11. **What Could You Ask an Adult?** (3 minutes). Let's make a list of the questions that you could ask adults—parents, grandparents, aunts, uncles, or teachers—about divorce and families.

*Processing* (5 minutes)

12. It is helpful to talk to people, especially adults, and to ask them things if we are not sure. Sometimes we blame ourselves for things that are not our fault; others can help us to see that something is not our fault. Let's everyone go around and finish the sentence: *One person whom kids could talk to if they thought it was their fault would be XXX, and one question they could ask them is XXX.*

*Closing* (3 minutes)

13. Sing **"And I Need A Lot Of Love."**

*Homework*

14. Tell the children that next week is your last week of group and to think about what they have learned.
15. Ask the children to listen to a song when they feel down this week.

# 2-A

# Feelings About the Divorce

## GOALS FOR THE SESSION

1. To discuss what feelings are and why they aren't right or wrong— they just are.
2. To help identify some feelings related to the divorce.
3. To introduce the idea that it is good to talk about feelings.

## MATERIALS

- Banner with group name and ground rules hanging on the wall
- "If You Believe In You" tape (specifically "Everybody Needs A Friend" and "Divorce" songs)
- A feeling chart or a list of feeling words
- Large notepad and markers

## GROUP SESSION

*Warm-Up* (6 minutes)

1. Play the **"Divorce"** song (3 minutes).

2. What feelings did they sing about in the song? (3 minutes).

*Working Activities* (31 minutes)

3. **Feelings** (5 minutes). What are feelings? How do you know when you have a feeling? Why do you have feelings? Make sure that they understand that feelings are internal, that different people have different feelings, that your body gives you clues that you have a feeling (tenseness, feeling in stomach, etc.), and that feelings help us to know and to understand ourselves.

4. Let's name all the feelings we can think of. Introduce a feeling chart or list as they finish their list (5 minutes).

5. **Feelings About Divorce** (10 minutes). Now let's go through and circle all the different feelings that children may have when their parents divorce or separate. Make sure that they circle some positive feelings as well as negative ones. Have them state why a child might have that feeling.

6. **Why Are There So Many Different Feelings?** (3 minutes). Let's talk about why there are so many

different feelings. One reason is that each divorce and family situation is a little different, and so everyone may have different feelings. One child may be very sad, whereas another child may feel angry. Another reason is that feelings change over time. At first you may be sad, but later on you may be relieved that there is no more fighting. Another reason is that feelings aren't right or wrong; they just are. It is OK to have all of these feelings. Where you get into trouble sometimes is how you express them. If you are angry, it is OK to say "I'm angry" but not to hit someone (3 minutes).

7. **Ways to Express Feelings** (8 minutes). Let's now talk about ways to express these different feelings. Point to different feelings and have the children act out first an inappropriate expression of the feeling and then an appropriate way to express the feeling. Encourage them to yell and jump and shout the inappropriate way and then have them repeat the appropriate ways until they are really appropriate (use feeling words and "I" statements that are expressive but not accusing).

*Processing* (5 minutes)

8. Feelings are always OK. When children experience divorce, they have lots of different feelings. Let's everyone go around and finish the sentence: *One feeling that children often have when their parents separate or divorce is* XXX.

*Closing* (3 minutes)

9. Play **"Everybody Needs A Friend"** and have them sing the refrain: **You gotta find somebody to talk to. You're gonna need somebody to talk to. You gotta tell somebody what you've been through. Everybody needs a friend.**

# 2-B

# The Emotional Process of Divorce

## GOALS FOR THE SESSION

1. To explain the emotional process of divorce.
2. To identify ways that both parents and children go through the emotional process.
3. To identify ways to cope with the stages of the process.

## MATERIALS

- Banner with group name and ground rules hanging on the wall
- "If You Believe In You" tape (specifically the "Divorce" and "So Am I" songs)
- Large notepad and markers
- Copies of the handout The Emotional Process of Divorce for each child

## GROUP SESSION

*Warm-Up* (6 minutes)
1. Play the **"Divorce"** song (3 minutes).

2. **Identification of Different Feelings** (3 minutes). Cory sang about a lot of different feelings in this song when he found out that his parents were going to get divorced. What were they? Shocked, could not believe, angry, sad.

*Working Activities* (31 minutes)
3. **Explanation of the Emotional Process of Divorce** (12 minutes). Cory had lots of different feelings about the divorce. Kids have lots of different feelings and parents do, too. People have actually studied the feelings and come up with a pattern of the feelings. They talk about them as steps. Let's talk about them for a minute. Write the steps on the notepad as you talk. Each step has feelings and thoughts that go along with it.

| FEELING | EXAMPLES OF THOUGHTS |
|---|---|
| Denial | Can't believe that the divorce or separation is happening. May pretend that everything is OK. Doesn't tell anyone that parents are separated. This can't be happening. I don't believe it. They always fight and then get back together. |

| FEELING | EXAMPLES OF THOUGHTS |
|---|---|
| Anger | Anger at the situation and at your parents. I hate them both. They are ruining my life. |
| Bargaining | Tries to make a deal to get parents back together again. I'll be good if you get back together. God, I will never lie again if they get back together. In **"Is It My Fault?"** Cory says, I'll try to change and rearrange my room if they will stop acting so strange. I'll ask Santa to get my parents back together. |
| Depression | Feels sad and hopeless about the situation. I am so sad. I don't want to do anything. I don't want to eat. I want to sleep all the time. Nothing seems like fun. |
| Acceptance | Accepts the situation. I accept the situation. It isn't exactly what I want, but I can live with it. I can't change the situation. I can only change my reaction to it. I would rather my parents be married to each other, but their new partners are OK. |

Sometimes you can be in a step for a long time, and sometimes in 1 day, you can be in several steps. It usually takes a couple of years (3 to 6) for both children and parents to get to the step of acceptance.

4. **Identification of the Thoughts That Go Along With the Emotional Steps** (10 minutes). Pass out the handout. Let's individually write down examples of thoughts that go along with each step. Then we'll read them out loud and guess which step they belong to.

5. **Which Step Is This?** (9 minutes). After everyone has completed the handout, randomly read a statement and have the group guess which step it is and say why.

*Processing* (5 minutes)

6. We have talked a lot today about the thoughts and feelings for each emotional step. Now let's take a minute and share things that children can do to feel better when they are in one of these stages. Let's everyone go around and finish the sentence: *One thing that kids can do to feel better when they are feeling XXX is XXX.*

*Closing* (3 minutes)

7. Play **"So Am I"** and sing along.

# The Emotional
# Process of Divorce

*STEP*          *THOUGHTS*

**Denial**      1.  I'll just pretend that they are still together and no one will know.

                2.

                3.

**Anger**       1.  I hate them both for ruining my life.

                2.

                3.

**Bargaining**  1.  Santa, please get my parents back together for my Christmas present.

                2.

                3.

**Depression**  1.  Nothing is fun.

                2.

                3.

**Acceptance**  1.  I wish my parents were still married but at least their new partners aren't witches.

                2.

                3.

# 2-C

# Sad Feelings About the Divorce or Separation

## GROUP SESSION

*Warm-Up* (4 minutes)

1. Let's listen to the **"I Worry"** song and identify things that a child whose parents are separating or divorcing might be sad about. Play the **"I Worry"** song.

*Working Activities* (33 minutes)

2. **Why Are Kids Sad?** (6 minutes). Let's list things that children of divorce might be sad about. (List on the notepad in the left-hand column, leaving room for three other columns: other feelings, what is making you feel this way, and what can be done to make you feel differently.)

3. **How to Deal With Sadness** (12 minutes). Sometimes it is hard to talk about being sad. And it is important to figure out a couple of things before you can do something to change the situation. You need to figure out why you are feeling a certain way, what specifically is making you feel that way, how long you have been feeling that way, and what would help you to feel differently. So let's go through our list and fill in these other columns. Let's each take a column so the first person identifies any other possible feelings for the first situation, the second person identifies what is making you feel that way, and the third person identifies what can be done to change the situation. Continue until all columns are full, with you filling in the tough columns—perhaps what can be done to change the situation the first time, if needed.

43

4. **Role-Play Practice** (15 minutes). These are great ideas, but sometimes it helps even more to act them out. So let's use the puppets to act out some of the ways to talk about being sad and figuring out why you are sad and what to do about it. Now let's practice some of these strategies. Let's act out some situations with bad stuff. Ask children to volunteer to pick a situation and give a little background (tell them it can be make believe or real and they don't need to tell which) and then assign puppets and characters to other children to act out. Have one puppet talk to another puppet about feeling sad; the second puppet should help the first puppet talk about being sad and what they can do. (Leader may want to model being the second puppet in the first role-play). Each role-play can be 3 minutes, with 2 minutes afterward to talk about what they saw and what they learned. Emphasize the different ways to express feelings ("I" statements, feeling words, the specific incident that they don't like, and what they want to happen to change it).

*Processing* (5 minutes)

5. It is important to remember that when you are sad, your feelings are telling you something. You must figure out why you are sad and what you can do to make the situation different so you feel better. Talking to someone is a good way to help figure out why you are sad and what you can do about it. Let's remind ourselves about what can make us sad and what we can do about it. Let's everyone go around and finish the sentence: *One reason why children of divorce might feel sad is XXX, and one thing they can do is XXX.*

*Closing* (3 minutes)

6. Play **"Everybody Needs A Friend"** and sing along.

# 2-D

# Feeling Angry About the Divorce

## GROUP SESSION

*Warm-Up* (8 minutes)

1. Play the **"Divorce"** song (3 minutes).

2. There are lots of feelings in the **"Divorce"** song. One of them is being angry. What are some times when Kelly and Cory might have been angry about the divorce? Let's make a list of different things that make children of divorce angry. Make a list on the notepad (5 minutes).

*Working Activities* (29 minutes)

3. **Ways to Deal With Anger** (8 minutes). Let's pick one of the things on our list and talk about different ways to deal with that situation. Choose a relatively simple situation. Ask the children to brainstorm ways to deal with the situation. Emphasize that it is OK to be angry but it is not OK to hit or yell at another person to express the anger. Also emphasize that there are two major ways to cope: (a) to talk with someone outside of the situation to vent and to get some ideas on how to solve the problem and (b) to talk with the person you are angry at directly. Sometimes you will need to do both to resolve the situation, and sometimes only one way is needed.

4. **Role-Play Practice** (21 minutes). OK, now let's act out some of the other situations and some ways to deal with them. Ask each child to pick a situation

and give a little background (tell them it can be make believe or real and they don't need to tell which) and then assign puppets and characters to other children to act out. Each role-play can be 3 minutes, with 2 minutes afterward to talk about what they saw and what they learned. Emphasize the different ways to express feelings ("I" statements, feeling words, the specific incident that makes you angry, and what you want to be different).

*Processing* (5 minutes)

5. There are lots of ways to deal with anger. It is OK to be angry but not to hurt someone when you express your anger. Let's everyone go around and finish the sentence: *One situation about the divorce that might make a kid angry is XXX, and one way to deal with it is XXX.*

*Closing* (3 minutes)

6. Play the **"Divorce"** song and sing along.

# 3-A

# Communication Skills

## GROUP SESSION

### GOALS FOR THE SESSION

1. To teach basic communication skills.
2. To practice communication skills related to divorce situations.

### MATERIALS

- Banner with group name and ground rules hanging on the wall
- "If You Believe In You" tape (specifically "Casey The Clown" and "Everybody Needs A Friend" songs)
- Large notepad and markers
- Puppets

*Warm-Up* (5 minutes)

1. Play **"Casey The Clown"** (3 minutes).

2. In this song, Casey is having trouble at home, but instead of talking about it, he is the class clown, always telling jokes and getting in trouble. He is not communicating to his parents, his friends, or his teachers about what he is thinking or feeling. We hope that he told Mr. Conley what he was feeling because it is so important to talk to people (2 minutes).

*Working Activities* (32 minutes)

3. Communication is important to make us feel better and to help keep relationships. People need to know what we think, feel, and want in order to understand us. People aren't mind readers, so we have to tell them what we want and feel. Today we are going to talk about and then practice how to communicate our feelings and thoughts. It is important to communicate what we like just as much as what we don't like, so let's start with that.

4. **Positive Communication** (5 minutes). Good communication is easy, and there is a kind of formula to follow to do it. Let's think of it in terms of three steps, and let's start in terms of positive communication—things that feel good or are going well.

   **Step 1**: Who wants it? Or thinks? Or feels? I do. So say "I" clearly. I want . . . I like . . . I think . . . I feel . . .

Let's all go around and say something with an "I" statement: either I want, I like, I think, or I feel.

**Step 2**: About what? What do you want? Or think? Or feel? Be clear. I want to change seats with you. . . . I think that this is a great song. . . . I like it when you smile at me. . . . I feel happy when I come home and my Mom is there.

Let's all go around and say something with an "I" statement and about what. Choose a different one than you did last time: I want . . . I think . . . I like . . . I feel . . .

5. **Negative Communication** (7 minutes). Great. Now let's go a little further. Sometimes we don't like things or feel sad or have to tell people things that are hard to say. We do Steps 1 and 2 just like before, so let's try them again.

**Step 1**: Let's start with the "I" statements. I don't want . . . I don't think . . . I don't like.

**Step 2**: Now let's add about what. Things like I don't want to stay home alone on Friday night. … I feel sad when I have to say good-bye to my Mom on Sunday. . . . I don't think that it is a good idea for me to give my Mom messages for you. . . . I don't like it when my Mom and Dad fight in front of me.

OK, now let's have you try it. I don't want . . . I feel . . . I don't like . . . I don't think . . .

**Step 3**: A new step. What do you want to happen to change the situation? I don't want to stay home alone on Friday night. I want an adult to stay with me. . . . I feel sad when I have to say good-bye to my Mom on Sunday. I would like for her to call me when she gets home so I can say good-bye again. . . . I don't think it is a good idea for me to give my Mom messages for you. You could call her on the phone to talk with her. . . . I don't like it when my Mom and Dad fight in front of me. I will leave the room when they do.

OK, now let's have you try it. Remember three steps (write them on the notepad):

"I" statement

About what?

What do you want to be different?

6. **Role-Play Practice** (20 minutes). Now let's practice some of these strategies. Let's act out some situations where you need to tell someone that you don't like something; don't want something; or feel sad, mad, or angry. Ask children to vol-

unteer to pick a situation and give a little background (tell them it can be make believe or real and they don't need to tell which) and then assign puppets and characters to other children to act out. Each role-play can be 4 minutes, with 2 minutes afterward to talk about what they saw and what they learned. Emphasize the different ways to express feelings ("I" statements, feeling words, the specific incident that they don't like, and what they want to happen to change it).

*Processing* (5 minutes)

7. We just practiced the negative communication. Now let's practice the positive. It is really helpful to know what things we do that people like and how we are helpful to others. So let's end with positive statements to people in the group. Let's take turns looking at the person to the right of you and making a positive statement. Remember the three steps and look at the notepad if you need to. *I like it when you XXX. I feel XXX when you XXX. I think it is good that you XXX.*

*Closing* (3 minutes)

8. Play **"Everybody Needs A Friend"** and sing along.

# 3-B

# Nonverbal Communication

## GOALS FOR THE SESSION

1. To identify ways that people communicate nonverbally.
2. To identify the messages that are being communicated nonverbally.
3. To practice verbalizing nonverbal messages.

## MATERIALS

- Banner with group name and ground rules hanging on the wall
- "If You Believe In You" tape (specifically the "I Tried" song)
- Large notepad and markers
- Nonverbal Feeling Charades handout cut into individual slips of paper

## GROUP SESSION

*Warm-Up* (6 minutes)

1. **Introduction to Nonverbal Communication** (2 minutes). Today we are going to talk about how we communicate nonverbally as well as verbally to our friends, parents, teachers, and peers. What do we mean by verbal communication? What do we mean by nonverbal communication? Emphasize that with both, we are communicating that we are telling someone something. My favorite example of nonverbal communication is in one of Dan's songs called **"I Tried."** Actually there are two examples: He expresses that he doesn't like his mother's new boyfriend and his father's new girlfriend. Let's listen and see what he does.

2. Play **"I Tried"** (3 minutes).

3. **Dan's feelings** (1 minute). What does Dan do nonverbally to express his feelings? What do you think he was trying to communicate?

*Working Activities* (31 minutes)

4. **Nonverbal Feeling Charades** (20 minutes). Let's play a game called Nonverbal Feeling Charades. Here's a pile of papers, each with a feeling on it. Let's take turns picking a piece of paper and then **nonverbally** acting out the feeling on the paper. **No words.**

5. **Processing of Game** (5 minutes). How easy was it to guess the feelings? Which ones did we have trouble with? Do you see how sometimes you may be trying to communicate one feeling nonverbally and someone thinks you are feeling differently?

When have you tried to communicate one feeling and someone else thought that you were feeling differently? What happened? How did you feel then?

6. **Verbally Expressing Nonverbal Messages** (6 minutes). Let's work on some of the times that you just mentioned when you were feeling one thing and other people thought you were feeling something else. What could you say in these situations to make your feelings known accurately to other people? Go through the situations that were identified in Number 5 above and make suggestions about how to verbally express the feelings.

*Processing* (5 minutes)

7. It is often difficult to express your feelings just nonverbally. People are often mistaken or unsure about what you are feeling when you don't say something. Let's everyone go around and finish the sentence: *One feeling that is sometimes hard to recognize in other people is XXX because XXX.*

*Closing* (3 minutes)

8. Play **"I Tried"** and sing along.

# Nonverbal Feeling Charades

| | | |
|---|---|---|
| Feeling Happy | Feeling Sad | Feeling Down |
| Feeling Excited | Feeling Irritable | Feeling Tired |
| Feeling Angry | Feeling Embarrassed | Feeling Hopeful |
| Feeling Lovestruck | Feeling Confident | Feeling Jealous |
| Feeling Lonely | Feeling Anxious | Feeling Cautious |
| Feeling Confused | Feeling Ashamed | Feeling Overwhelmed |
| Feeling Shy | Feeling Frightened | Feeling Frustrated |

# 4

# How to Cope
# With Parental Fighting

## GOALS FOR THE SESSION

1. To discuss reasons why people (especially parents) fight.
2. To discuss ways to cope with fighting.
3. To practice ways to cope with fighting.

## MATERIALS

- Banner with group name and ground rules hanging on the wall
- "If You Believe In You" tape (specifically the "Bad Mood" and "So Am I" songs)
- Large notepad and markers
- **Ways to Cope** handout cut into individual slips of paper
- Puppets

## GROUP SESSION

*Warm-Up* (7 minutes)

1. Play **"Bad Mood"** (3 minutes).

2. **What Do People Do When They Are in a Bad Mood?** (2 minutes). What are some of the things that people do in the song **"Bad Mood?"** Answers: They slam the door, talk fast, give orders, don't notice how others are feeling, are sarcastic, talk back, and say "get out."

3. **What Else Do People Do When They Are in a Bad Mood?** (2 minutes). Answers: yell, fight, etc.

*Working Activities* (30 minutes)

4. **Reasons Parents Fight** (5 minutes). One of the reasons why people get divorced is because they can't get along and they fight all the time. That is hard for them and hard for their children, too. What kinds of things do parents fight about? Make a list on the notepad.

5. **Feelings** (3 minutes). Sometimes parents still fight after they get divorced because they still can't agree on important issues. So it is important for us to talk about ways to cope with times when parents might fight. What kinds of feelings might Kelly and Cory have when their parents still fight?

6. **Ways to Cope** (5 minutes). What kinds of things could Kelly and Cory do to cope when their parents fight? Make a list on the notepad.

7. **Role-Play Practice** (17 minutes). These are great ideas, but sometimes it helps even more to act them out. So let's use the puppets to act out some of the ways to cope when parents fight. Let's practice some of these strategies. Let's act out some situations when parents fight. Ask children to volunteer to be two parents and ask them to fight (let them pick out puppets), and then ask two children at a time to be Kelly and Cory (let them pick out puppets). Each role-play can be 3 minutes. Take turns being the parents and the children.

*Processing* (5 minutes)

8. It is very hard when people whom you love don't get along. It is even harder when they fight in front of you. Today we talked about some good ways to cope when this happens. Let's everyone go around and finish the sentence: *One thing that children of divorce can do to make themselves feel better when their parents fight is XXX.* (If they can't come up with something, have them choose a slip of paper cut from the **Ways to Cope** handout and have them say why this would be helpful.)

*Closing* (3 minutes)

9. Play **"So Am I"** and sing the chorus.

# Ways to Cope

Talk with parent

Talk with friend

Talk to an adult (counselor, family member, teacher, family friend)

Write down your feelings

Listen to one of Dan's songs

Talk to a friend whose parents are divorced

Talk to an adult whose parents are divorced

Ask someone what they would do if they felt the way you do

Imagine yourself saying "Stop. I don't want to hear this."

Say "Stop. I don't want to hear this."

Tell one of your parents when you are alone with them that you don't like it when they fight and could they not do that in front of you.

# 5-A

# What Do All the Big Words Mean for Me?

## GROUP SESSION

*Warm-Up* (10 minutes)

1. Play the **"Divorce"** song (3 minutes).

2. **Words Related to Divorce** (7 minutes). Make a list of divorce-related terms. If you listened to the song, Dan sings about divorce and about how he found out that his parents were getting divorced. Lots of children have to learn a whole new vocabulary when they find out about divorce. Let's make a list of all the words that children of divorce have to learn. Add to the list if the following words aren't on the list: *divorce, guardian ad litem, hearing/trial, judge, mediation, residential parent, legal guardian, separation agreement, shared parenting, support,* and *visitation.* Add any other terms that you think might be relevant on the basis of individual children's situations.

*Working Activities* (28 minutes)

3. **Definitions** (15 minutes). Today we are going to talk about all these new words and make sure that we understand what they really mean. Go through the list that the children have just generated, and with their help, define all the words on the list. Use the Layperson's Description of Legal Terms that follows this session as a definitional guide.

4. **What Happens in Court?** (13 minutes). Let's act out what we think happens in a court of law for a divorce

56

to happen and then let's talk about how accurate it really is. The leader should be the judge, who directs the whole role-play through questions. Assign people to puppets for the mother, father, lawyer for mother, lawyer for father, son, and daughter. Direct the role-play based on the following outline: Judge explains what will happen in the court proceedings that day. He or she will be gathering some information to help decide where the children should live. Ask the parents questions such as, Why should the children live with you? How will you make sure that they eat three meals a day, get to school on time, and go to bed at a reasonable time? Who will watch them while you work? Ask the lawyers questions such as, What happens if Mom and Dad can't agree on custody? What is the lawyer's role? What is reasonable for visitation? How is child support decided? What kinds of questions do children get asked? Will they be asked to choose between their mother and father?

*Processing* (4 minutes)

5.  There are lots of big words related to divorce, and it is helpful to understand what they mean. Sometimes if we don't know what a word means, we don't understand what is happening, and it is scary. And it is hard to talk about, too. Let's each say one word that all kids should know what it means and then the next person tells what it means. Let's go all around the circle.

*Closing* (3 minutes)

6.  Music makes people feel good. So let's sing as we end today.

7.  Play **"Divorce"** and sing along.

# List of Legal Terms

**Affidavit**—a sworn statement in writing.

**Agreed Entry**—a document filed by attorney when both parties come to an agreement on some issue.

**Allegation**—a statement which is stated as fact without proof.

**Allocation Parental Rights and Responsibilities**—court determination as to which party will be the residential parent and which parent will be the nonresidential parent, or as to whether the parties will participate in shared parenting.

**Appraiser**—a person who determines a monetary value on your assets (house, property, furniture, household goods).

**Assets, Nonmarital**—those items which were brought to the marriage by the parties which have not been altered or comingled. Also includes possessions held specifically by one party, e.g., inheritances, trust funds.

**Comingled**—mixed together.

**Decree**—final order of the court dissolving the marriage contract. Must be entered in court's journal before marriage has officially ended.

**Defendant**—the person who may answer the filing by the other party in a court case; in a divorce, usually the spouse (plaintiff).

**Discovery**—the process whereby attorneys collect from each party information on martial assets, i.e., funds on deposit, pension plans, insurance policies, appraisals.

**Dissolution**—a legal process to end the marriage contract in which two parties reach a settlement on all issues in the divorce before filing. Grounds are irreconcilable. No fault is found.

**Division of Child Support**—the country office through which support payments must be made.

**Divorce**—a legal process to end the marriage contract. Parties cannot make a decision and court must decide for them. Divorce is granted to one party, but this has no bearing on court decisions. Must allege and prove grounds.

**Emancipated**—a child who reaches age 18 or completes high school, whichever is later; marries; enters the armed forces; or is financially independent is no longer viewed by the court as his or her parents' legal responsibility.

**Grounds**—basis for the divorce which must be alleged in the divorce court. Three most commonly used are gross neglect, extreme cruelty, or living separate and apart without cohabitation for 1 year.

**Guardian ad Litem**—an attorney appointed by court to represent the interests of the child.

**Hearing, Merits (Dissolution)**—a very brief session in which both parties must appear before the judge to verify their separation agreement and to state the agreement is fair.

**Hearing, Merits (Divorce)**—a very brief session in which the plaintiff tells the judge in a few words the grounds for divorce. The plaintiff must have a witness to confirm these grounds.

**Hearing, Property**—presentation of evidence on the identification and value of assets leading to an order by a referee for a fair division.

**Hearing, Temporary**—presentation of evidence on temporary custody, support, and/or alimony until the final order of the court has been made.

**Hearing/Trial**—presentation of evidence or arguments by both parties through attorneys to a referee or judge in order for the court to make a decision concerning the issues.

**Journalized**—when the court's order is made formal by recording it in the court's journal (see Decree).

**Judge**—elected official who presides over objections, hearings, custody trials, and merit hearings.

**Jurisdiction**—the limits or territory (e.g., geographical location) over which the court has authority. If divorce is granted in a particular county, court retains its authority over it unless a change is requested.

**Liquid Assets**—those assets which can readily be converted to cash, e.g., stocks, bonds, savings accounts.

**Mediation**—a process whereby a neutral third party (a mediator) assists the parties to develop their own agreement without the court's intervention (in divorce, i.e., decisions concerning property, allocation of parental rights and responsibilities, support, and/or spousal support).

**Objections**—a written notice of alleged errors made by referee (concerning a specific decision made during hearing) requesting review by judge.

**Parenting Investigation**—(occurs only when the couple cannot agree on custody) a process which takes an average of 3 months during which a court-assigned specialist explores the divorcing parents' character, family relations, past conduct, capacity to provide for children's physical and emotional needs in order to recommend which parent shall have the parental rights and responsibilities for the care of the children (specifically and primarily, what is in the children's best interest).

**Parenting Specialist**—a court employee designated to conduct the parenting investigation (see Parenting Investigation).

**Pendente Lite**—pending litigation; a court order that is in effect until the final order of the court has been made. Often order is result of temporary hearing.

**Plaintiff**—the person who is filing for divorce or allocation of parental rights and responsibilities.

**Postdecree Motion**—any legal action which is filed after the divorce or dissolution has been finalized.

**Poundage**—presently a 2% surcharge made by the court which is added to ordered child support and/or alimony to cover administrative costs.

**Pretrial**—a conference between the referee and the attorneys of both parties, usually in regard to custody or property, to identify those issues on which there is agreement, identify what evidence is still required, and how long trial will take.

**Pro se**—a person proceeding in court without an attorney.

**Referee**—a lawyer appointed by the judge and given authority by state law to act in his or her place in examining evidence and making decisions. Presides over temporary, property, and support hearings and any other hearings requested by the judge. Referee orders are subject to review by judge within 14 days of the date of ruling.

**Residency Requirement**—must have lived in the state a certain number of months before divorce or dissolution (differs in each state).

**Residential Parent and Legal Custodian**—a term used to define the parent having decision-making responsibility for the child or children who are under age 18 (see also Shared Parenting).

**Separation Agreement**—a written contract between the parties providing for the settlement of such issues as allocation of parental rights and responsibilities, visitation, distribution of property, allocation of debts, spousal support, and child support.

**Shared Parenting**—a term used when both parents share legal responsibility for all decisions made concerning the children. A written agreement must be submitted to the courts covering the child's residence and his time spent with each parent, support arrangements, health coverage, discipline, transportation to school, religious training, and visitation. Plans vary widely. Some parents may divide child's residence between them 90/10, 50/50, or other ways.

**Spousal Support**—previously termed alimony. A court-ordered payment by one party to the other for purposes of discharging the obligation to support or maintain based on various statutory criteria.

**Support**—a regular payment from one parent to the other to help share the costs of raising children. Can be paid by father or mother.

**Support Counselor**—a staff member of the court who assists with support problems after the divorce or dissolution has been finalized.

**Trial**—(see Hearing)

**Visitation**—specified time for the noncustodial parent to visit alone with his or her children.

# 5-B

# Visitation

## GROUP SESSION

*Warm-Up* (8 minutes)

1. Play **"And I Need A Lot Of Love"** (3 minutes).

2. Dan is singing about how we all need a lot of love. Families give us lots of love. How do they do that? Let's talk for a minute about different ways that families give and show love. Emphasize that they hug, say I love you, provide support, listen, and play. Emphasize positive times as well as support for crises (5 minutes).

*Working Activities* (29 minutes)

3. **Visitation and Custody** (15 minutes). One of the hardest things for children of divorce is that they no longer have both parents in their home with them. Everybody's situation is a little different in how they spend time with both parents. Sometimes the courts and judges get involved and say, "You will live with your father but see your mother every Wednesday and every other weekend." Other times moms and dads are able to work it out as to when they see their children. Some children live with one parent and see the other parent on weekends. Some children don't see the other parent at all. Some children split their time between both parents or live with their grandparents or other family members. Let's spend a few minutes and talk about what your visitation arrangement is. If you know what the court has determined

about your visitation arrangement or what was written in your parents' divorce, you can say that, and then if it is different, tell us what actually happens. (Note to leader: Check the background information that you collected to see what the parent has indicated so you are prepared with the child's responses and you have some sense of the accuracy of what the child reports.)

4. **Positives and Negatives** (7 minutes). Label the notepad with Visitation and then columns for Positives and Negatives. Let's now think about what we have heard and make a list of all the positives and negatives about these visitation situations. You can talk about your situation or somebody else's. Let's start with some of the problems with visitation.

5. Now let's think about this from a different perspective. What are some of the good things about visitation? What happens now that didn't happen before the divorce? (7 minutes).

*Processing* (5 minutes)

6. Visitation for children is usually hard in the beginning. But both good and bad things usually happen with visitation. Let's everyone go around and finish the sentence: *One problem with visitation is XXX, but one good thing that happens for kids with visitation is XXX.*

*Closing* (3 minutes)

7. Play **"And I Need A Lot Of Love"** and sing along.

# 6

# Some Ways to Cope With Parents Who Don't Live Together

### GOALS FOR THE SESSION

1. To identify problem situations associated with parents who don't live together.
2. To suggest ways to deal with these situations.
3. To practice potential solutions.

### MATERIALS

- Banner with group name and ground rules hanging on the wall
- "If You Believe In You" Tape (specifically the "Bad Mood" song)
- Large notepad and markers
- Puppets

## GROUP SESSION

*Warm-Up* (5 minutes)

1. I am going to play the **"Bad Mood"** song. Let's listen carefully to what Dan is singing about with regard to his father and his mother.

2. Play **"Bad Mood"** (3 minutes).

3. Did you hear what Dan says to his father on the phone? "Gee, Dad, if you are so keen on what Mom says, how come you aren't living here?" Sometimes it is hard for children to understand how parents can still be parents **together** if they don't want to stay married. And sometimes it is hard for parents to be parents **together** when they are divorced (2 minutes).

*Working Activities* (32 minutes)

4. **Problems** (10 minutes). Let's talk about some of the problems that happen because your parents don't live together and/or don't get along. Emphasize things such as they let the children do different things (curfews, rules), they fight in front of the kids, they say mean things about the other person, they ask the child to relay messages to the other person, and they get mad if the child talks about the other parent (or new stepparent). Write the problems down on the notepad, leaving room for another column to be added to later.

5. **Solutions** (5 minutes). Sometimes it is much easier to solve someone else's problem. So let's look at our

63

list and note which things we mentioned. Then let's take turns and go up and point out something that you didn't say and state a way to solve that problem. Keep going until all the problems have been solved. (Note to leader: You can fill in any remaining ones.)

6. **Role-Play Practice** (17 minutes). Now let's practice some of these strategies. Let's act out some of the other situations and some ways to deal with them. Ask children to volunteer to pick a situation and give a little background (tell them it can be make believe or real and they don't need to tell which) and then assign puppets and characters to other children to act out. Each role-play can be 4 minutes, with 2 minutes afterward to talk about what they saw and what they learned. Emphasize the different ways to express feelings ("I" statements, feeling words, the specific incident that makes you angry, and what you want to be different).

*Processing* (5 minutes)

7. It is important to realize that new families need time to get adjusted to each other. It is important to talk to each other and spend time together to get to know each other and to learn how to get along. Let's everyone go around and finish the sentence: *One problem that can happen to children of divorce when their parents don't live together is XXX, and one way they can cope with it is XXX.*

*Closing* (3 minutes)

8. Play **"Bad Mood"** and sing along.

# Maintaining Parental Relationships

## GROUP SESSION

*Warm-Up* (5 minutes)

1. Play **"Bad Mood"** and sing along (3 minutes).

2. **Changes When Parents Don't Live Together** (2 minutes). It is hard for everyone when parents don't live together. Dan has a great line in the song **"Bad Mood"** when he says to his Dad, "So if you are so keen on what Mom says, why aren't you living here anymore?" Mom and Dad don't get along, which is why they got divorced, but they still need to work together as parents to take care of the children. But things change when you don't live with both parents every day.

*Working Activities* (32 minutes)

3. **What Were Your Parents Like When They Both Lived With You?** (7 minutes). Let's think for a minute about what it was like when your parents lived together. For those of you who can't remember, try to imagine what it would be like. Let's go around and each say: *One thing that a Mom might say to a child on a typical day when both parents live with their children would be XXX.*

Now let's go around and each say: *One thing that a Dad might say to a child on a typical day when both parents live with their children would be XXX.*

(Point out any similarities in themes, and try to notice things that they probably wouldn't say if the parents weren't together.)

4. **What Are Your Parents Like When They Both Live Apart?** (7 minutes). Now let's go around and each say: *One thing that a Dad might say to a child on a typical day when both parents DON'T live with their children would be XXX.*

   Now let's go around and each say: *One thing that a Mom might say to a child on a typical day when both parents DON'T live with their children would be XXX.*

   Ask how their answers are different. Did parents take on different roles? What did they do more of? Less of?

5. **Problems With Current Relationships With the Parent You Don't Live With** (8 minutes). Let's make a list of the problems that happen when you live with only one parent. What happens to your relationship with the other parent? Make a list on the notepad.

6. **Making That Relationship Better** (10 minutes). Let's talk now about ways to make that relationship better. What can children of divorce do to keep in touch with that parent? Have a good time with them? Share day-to-day stuff with them? Go around and ask each child to say one thing that children of divorce could do. If they can't think of anything, ask them to draw a slip of paper cut from the **Ways to Make the Relationship Better** handout and say why that would make the relationship better.

*Processing* (5 minutes)

7. Relationships take a lot of time to develop and make them work. Your relationships with your father and mother changed when the divorce happened. It is time to now make it better. You are old enough to make changes and make things the way you want them to be. Let's everyone go around and finish this sentence: *One thing that children of divorce can do to stay close to the parent they don't live with is XXX.*

*Closing* (3 minutes)

8. Play **"And I Need A Lot Of Love"** and sing along.

# Ways to Make
# the Relationship Better

Call the person just to say hi.

Call the person to tell them something funny that happened that day.

Call the person to tell them that you love them.

Call the person to tell them that you miss them.

E-mail the person just to say hi.

E-mail the person to tell them something funny that happened that day.

E-mail the person to tell them that you love them.

E-mail the person to tell them that you miss them.

Ask the person to help you with your homework or a special project.

Ask the person for advice about a problem with a friend.

Ask the person to tell you stories about when you were little.

Ask the person to tell you stories about when they were little.

Tell the person when they do something that you like.

Tell the person when they do something that you don't like, but nicely, and tell them that you still love them.

# 8-A

# Life Is Tough and Some Ways to Cope With It

**GOALS FOR THE SESSION**

1. To acknowledge some of the tough situations that occurred before parents got divorced or separated.
2. To suggest some ways to cope with difficult situations.

**MATERIALS**

- Banner with group name and ground rules hanging on the wall
- "If You Believe In You" tape (specifically the "So Am I" song)
- Worksheet entitled **Life Is Tough and So Am I**
- Crayons

## GROUP SESSION

*Warm-Up* (13 minutes)

1. Play the **"So Am I"** song and have the children sing along (3 minutes).

2. **Tough Stuff** (10 minutes). Dan says that "a lot of kids are having trouble at home and we all got together and had a pretty good cry." What kinds of stuff happens at home that makes it hard for kids? Let's talk about some of the things that happened before your parents separated or got divorced that were tough. Add to the list things such as parents fighting, one parent not being around much, parents yelling at the children, and parents crying.

*Working Activities* (25 minutes)

3. **Help With the Tough Stuff.** Let's talk today about some ways to help with the tough stuff. Here are some suggestions: Let's read them out loud and then color in each box. Hand out the sheet entitled **Life Is Tough and So Am I.** Read each box out loud, and then have them color in the box. Take about 4 minutes to color in each box.

*Processing* (4 minutes)

4. It is helpful to have a plan about what to do when we get scared or anxious or worried. Today we talked and colored about what to do when life is tough.

Let's try to come up with some new ideas as well as the ones we colored. Let's everyone go around and finish the sentence: *One thing that kids can do when life is tough is XXX.*

*Closing* (3 minutes)

5. Play **"So Am I"** and sing along.

# Life Is Tough and So Am I

HERE ARE SOME THINGS THAT I CAN DO WHEN LIFE IS TOUGH:

1. I CAN PLAY SONGS AND SING ALONG. WHAT SONG WOULD YOU SING?

2. I CAN TALK TO SOMEONE. WHO WOULD YOU TALK TO?

3. I CAN ASK SOMEONE FOR A HUG. WHO COULD GIVE YOU A HUG?

# 8-B

# Different Types of Families

## GOALS FOR THE SESSION

1. To emphasize that families may look different but they are all families.
2. To emphasize the importance of families in loving children and keeping them safe.
3. To emphasize the similarities between children's families.


## MATERIALS

- Banner with group name and ground rules hanging on the wall
- "If You Believe In You" tape (specifically And "I Need A Lot Of Love" song)
- Different Types of Families handout cut into individual slips of paper
- Large notepad and markers

## GROUP SESSION

*Review and Check-In* (8 minutes)

1. Play **"And I Need A Lot Of Love"** (3 minutes).

2. **We All Need a Lot of Love** (5 minutes). What is the theme of this song? All children, and all people, need a lot of love. And where do we get most of our love from? Our families. There are lots of different kinds of families, but they all give love and keep children safe. What do children need besides love? Make sure their list includes food, clothes, a place to live, help in getting to school, help in doing their homework, love, support, and someone to listen to.

*Working Activities* (29 minutes)

3. **Different Kinds of Families.** Today we are going to talk about the different kinds of families that there are. Let's play a little game. Let's see if we can name someone whom we know for each type of family. Let's make it fun by having different categories. Let's make three categories: people we know, TV and movie families, and book families. Put the three categories on a large notepad with the first category as type of family. Then make a pile in the center of the group with the slips of paper with the different types of family written on them. (Make sure that there is one slip of paper that fits each child's situation in the group. If not, add one to fit.) So let's start by picking a slip of paper out of the pile and then filling in each

of the three categories. (You can make teams and give points for each category.) Do as many of the slips of paper and categories as you can.

*Processing* (5 minutes)

4. There are lots of different types of families. The size or people don't matter; what matters is that there is a lot of love in each family. Let's everyone go around and finish the sentence: *One thing that I learned about families that I didn't know is XXX.*

*Closing* (3 minutes)

5. Play **"And I Need A Lot Of Love"** and sing along.

# Different Types of Families

Cut the list into individual slips. Put them in a pile. Have each child pick a slip and read it aloud. For each type of family, ask the children to name people whom they know that live in that type of family. Encourage them to include celebrities, TV and movie characters, and book characters. There is room at the bottom to add additional family configurations to make sure that all children in your group are represented.

| FAMILY CONFIGURATIONS | EXAMPLES |
|---|---|
| Mother with one or more children | Little Women <br> The Partridge Family <br> Jesse <br> One Fine Day <br> Mrs. Doubtfire <br> Rosie O'Donnell |
| Father with one or more children | Nancy Drew <br> Different Strokes <br> Silver Spoons <br> Who's the Boss? <br> Kramer vs. Kramer <br> One Fine Day <br> Michael Jackson <br> Pierce Brosnan <br> Courtship of Eddie's Father |
| Mother, grandmother, and grandfather with one or more children | Willie Wonka |
| Mother and grandmother with one or more children | Who's the Boss? <br> Lassie |
| Mother and grandfather with one or more children | Silver Spoons |
| Father and grandmother with one or more children | |
| Father and grandfather with one or more children | Safe Passages |
| Father, grandmother, and grandfather with one or more children | |
| Grandmother and grandfather with one or more children | Dawson's Creek |

| FAMILY CONFIGURATIONS | EXAMPLES |
|---|---|
| Grandmother with one or more children | |
| Grandfather with one or more children | Heidi |
| Mother and aunt with one or more children | |
| Father and aunt with one or more children | The Hogan Family<br>Andy Griffith Show |
| Father and uncle with one or more children | Full House<br>My Three Sons |
| Mother and boyfriend with one or more children | Once and Again |
| Aunt with one or more children | Fresh Prince of Bel Air<br>Auntie Mame |
| Uncle with one or more children | Family Affair |
| Foster parents with one or more children | Webster<br>Superman |
| Foster mother with one or more children | |
| Older sister with one or more children | Party of Five<br>Shania Twain |
| Older brother with one or more children | Party of Five |
| Foster father with one or more children | Al Pacino in<br>Author! Author |
| Father and girlfriend with one or more children | |
| Mother and stepfather with one or more children | The Brady Bunch |
| Father and stepmother with one or more children | The Brady Bunch<br>Silver Spoons |
| Mother, father, and children all live together | |
| Mother and girlfriend with one or more children | Ross's ex-wife on Friends |
| Father and boyfriend with one or more children | The Birdcage<br>Jody on Soap |
| Mother and female friend with one or more children | |
| Father and male friend with one or more children | My Two Dads |

*Session*

# 8-C

# New Traditions

## GOALS FOR THE SESSION

1. To identify some of the changes that have occurred as a result of the divorce or separation.
2. To express feelings of sadness and loss over some of the changes.
3. To brainstorm new traditions and identify positive aspects of some of the changes.

## MATERIALS

- Banner with group name and ground rules hanging on the wall
- "If You Believe In You" tape (specifically "I Am A Kid" song)
- Large notepad and markers
- Paper to draw on

## GROUP SESSION

*Warm-Up* (3 minutes)

1. Play the **"I Am A Kid"** song.

*Working Activities* (34 minutes)

2. **Old Traditions** (10 minutes). Today we are going to focus on traditions. Every family has its own traditions, things such as having Sunday dinners, eating a certain food on a child's birthday, or doing certain activities together. Let's think for a minute and share some traditions. (Model by sharing a few of your family traditions such as going bowling on Thanksgiving, eating shrimp on New Year's Day, and going for ice cream after a child's baseball game during the summer.) Let's everyone share a tradition that your family used to do before the divorce or separation.

3. **Current Traditions** (8 minutes). Now let's share current traditions that you really like and want to keep, ones that you do now with your mother, father, or other people in your family.

4. **New Traditions** (8 minutes). Now let's brainstorm new traditions that we would like to start now to make our new families special and fun. Let's draw our new traditions. Pass out paper.

5. Now let's share our new traditions (8 minutes).

75

*Processing* (5 minutes)

6. Traditions are so important to families. They give them time together and memories to share. It is important to end our time today by focusing on new traditions that we can work toward or keep going if we are already doing them. Let's everyone go around and finish the sentence: *One new tradition that I think would be great for children of divorce and their families is XXX.*

*Closing* (3 minutes)

7. Being a kid is a lot of fun and a great tradition. Play **"I Am A Kid"** and sing along.

# 9-A

# I Tried to Get My Mom and Dad Back Together Again

## GROUP SESSION

*Review and Check-In* (7 minutes)

1. Play the **"I Tried"** song (3 minutes).

2. What's the song about? Emphasize how hard it is for children to meet the new boyfriends and girlfriends when their parents start dating and how most children of divorce want their parents to get back together again (4 minutes).

*Working Activities* (30 minutes)

3. **Getting My Parents Back Together** (5 minutes). Today we are going to talk about the idea that just about everyone wants their parents to get back together. Let's start by talking about why this is so. Why do children want both of their parents to live in the same house?

4. **When My Parents Lived Together** (10 minutes). Now let's try to remember what it was like when both parents did live in the same house. (If some of the children don't remember, ask them to think about what it is like when their parents spend time together now.) Let's make a list of the good things and the not so good things about parents being together. Use the large notepad to record two columns: Good Things and Not So Good Things. Leave room between the columns so that you can add two more columns later.

5. **How Would It Be Different?** (5 minutes). Now let's work on both of those lists one at a time. Let's first talk about the Not So Good Things list. How would those be different if your parents got back together now? Do you think they would change? Emphasize that parents would probably still fight and argue about the same things because they are still different people.

6. **Good Things and How to Make Them Happen** (10 minutes). Now let's work on the Good Things list. Let's add another column called How to Make the Good Things Happen Now. How can this happen now? Let's brainstorm ways to make this happen. Let's also identify things that can't happen and maybe suggest other things that can take their place (e.g., Sunday dinner with both Mom and Dad being replaced with Sunday dinner with Mom and her family).

*Processing* (5 minutes)

7. When families change, some good things happen and some bad things happen. Let's everyone go around and finish the sentence: *One good thing that can still happen in my family is XXX.*

*Closing* (3 minutes)

8. Let's listen to **"I Tried"** again. Feel free to sing along. Let's listen at the end to the message: I let go and stopped trying to get my parents back together again.

# 9-B

# Still Trying to Get My Mom and Dad Back Together Again

## GROUP SESSION

*Review and Check-In* (7 minutes)

1. Play the **"I Tried"** song (3 minutes).

2. This song is about trying to get parents back together again. Why is that so important to children? (4 minutes).

*Working Activities* (28 minutes)

3. **Why Marriages Don't Work** (5 minutes). Let's talk about why marriages don't work. What kinds of reasons have you heard about why adults' marriages break up? Think about friends' parents, celebrities, and family members. Let's make as long a list as we can. Write the reasons down on the large notepad.

4. **How to Get My Parents Back Together** (8 minutes). The children in the song really wanted their parents to get back together again. Sometimes children come up with elaborate schemes about how to get their parents back together again. There have been a couple of movies and stories about this. Can anyone tell us about one? Let's be really silly for a few minutes and come up with some schemes to get our parents back together again.

5. OK. Now let's talk about whether these schemes would work based on our list of reasons why marriages break up. Would the schemes get them to talk

to each other? Respect each other? So they probably wouldn't work, would they? (5 minutes).

6. **Group Changes Since the Divorce** (10 minutes). At the end of the **"I Tried"** song, Dan sings about his parents being divorced and making the best of it. Sometimes there are advantages to parents being divorced, and it is important to recognize these when they happen. Things like parents not fighting anymore, time alone with Mom or Dad, more time with Mom or Dad, getting closer to sisters or brothers, and spending more time with grandparents or other relatives. Let's make a list of all the possible good things that could happen when parents get divorced. (Allow a few items like "more toys" and "Dad lets me do whatever I want," but try to keep them focused on quality time and less fighting.)

*Processing* (7 minutes)

7. Parents have lots of reasons for getting divorced, most of which have nothing to do with the children. Let's everyone go around and finish the sentence: *One reason that parents get divorced is* XXX (3 minutes).

8. Both good and bad things happen when parents divorce. Let's everyone go around and finish the sentence: *One good thing that usually happens for children when parents get divorced is* XXX (4 minutes).

*Closing* (3 minutes)

9. Let's listen to **"I Tried."** Let's sing along.

Session

# 9-C

# New People
# in Our Lives

## GROUP SESSION

*Warm-Up* (4 minutes)

1. Let's listen to what happens when somebody meets their Mom's new boyfriend and their Dad's new girl-friend. Play the **"I Tried"** song (3 minutes).

2. What happens when Dan meets the new boyfriend and girlfriend? Today we are going to talk about new people in our lives and about our new families (1 minute).

*Working Activities* (33 minutes)

3. **New People in Our Lives** (4 minutes). Dan is sing-ing about meeting his mother's boyfriend and his father's girlfriend. That is just the start of new rela-tionships. After parents divorce, they may remarry, live with new partners, or date new people. And these new people may already have children. Or your mother or father may have more children with their new partner. So there may be lots of new people in your life after a divorce. When we first started our group, we drew what our families looked like and who lived with us. Now let's draw Mom and Dad. Then let's add any other people such as new husbands or wives, or boyfriends or girlfriends, and their children if they have any. Pass out paper and markers.

4. **Who Has New People in Their Lives?** (6 minutes). Let's go around and share whose parents have boy-friends or girlfriends, or new husbands and wives,

**GOALS FOR THE SESSION**

1. To discuss what children's new families and relationships are like.
2. To identify problems with the new relation-ships and some ways to cope with them.
3. To identify positive aspects of these new relationships.

**MATERIALS**

- Banner with group name and ground rules hanging on the wall
- "If You Believe In You" tape (specifi-cally "I Tried" and "Everybody Needs A Friend" songs)
- Paper to draw on and markers
- Notepad
- Puppets

81

and children. Say something about where they live and how long they have been a part of your life.

5. Now let's talk about what it is like to have these new people in your life. Every new situation has both positives and negatives. So let's list some of the good things and some of the bad things that go along with these new relationships. List on the notepad under columns called Good Stuff and Bad Stuff; leave room under each phrase to add a solution later on (5 minutes).

6. **Solutions to the Bad Stuff** (5 minutes). Let's now think up some solutions to the bad stuff. Let's write some ideas under each thing that we listed under the bad stuff (5 minutes).

7. **Role-Play Practice** (13 minutes). These are great ideas, but sometimes it helps even more to act them out. So let's use the puppets to act some of these good ideas out. Now let's practice some of these strategies. Let's act out some situations with bad stuff. Ask children to volunteer to pick a situation and give a little background (tell them it can be make believe or real and they don't need to tell which) and then assign puppets and characters to other children to act out. Each role-play can be 4 minutes, with 2 minutes afterward to talk about what they saw and what they learned. Emphasize the different ways to express feelings ("I" statements, feeling words, the specific incident that they don't like, and what they want to happen to change it).

*Processing* (5 minutes)

8. We just focused on solutions to the bad stuff. Let's focus on the good things about these new people in our lives. Let's everyone go around and finish the sentence: *One good thing about new people in our lives is that XXX.*

*Closing* (3 minutes)

9. Play **"Everybody Needs A Friend"** and sing along.

# 9-D

# My Mom and Dad Are Dating Other People?

## GROUP SESSION

*Warm-Up* (9 minutes)

1. Let's listen to a song, **"I Tried."** Let's focus on what happens when the children in the song meet their Mom's new boyfriend and their Dad's new girlfriend (3 minutes).

2. **What Happened?** (2 minutes). So what happened with the new boyfriend? And what happened with the new girlfriend? Have the children tell you that in the song, the children spilled milk and wine on the new people.

3. How many of you have Moms or Dads with new boyfriends or girlfriends? New husbands or wives? (4 minutes).

*Working Activities* (29 minutes)

4. **Feelings About Parents' Boyfriends and Girlfriends** (2 minutes). The children in the song met the new boyfriend and girlfriend at a dinner. How do you think Kelly and Cory felt when they found out about the boyfriend and girlfriend?

5. What happened when you met the new boyfriends and girlfriends? How did you feel the first time you met? Use a feeling chart to help identify feelings (7 minutes).

6. **Getting Rid of Boyfriends or Girlfriends** (5 minutes). In the song, the children spilled milk and wine

83

on the new boyfriend and girlfriend to try to get them to go away so that they could get their parents back together again. Let's be silly for a few minutes. Sometimes it helps to just laugh about stuff and then deal with it. So let's be silly. What crazy things could you do to try to scare away these new boyfriends and girlfriends?

7. **How Would Your Parents Feel?** (3 minutes). Let's stop being silly now, although we had some really silly and crazy ideas. Let's talk about how your parents would feel if you did any of those things? Emphasize that they would be hurt, lonely, or sad.

8. Now let's think about why Moms and Dads might want girlfriends or boyfriends. Let's come up with some reasons why they would want to be in a romantic relationship (4 minutes).

9. **Ways to Cope With Boyfriends and Girlfriends** (8 minutes). So we have this dilemma. Children whose parents get divorced have all these feelings about new boyfriends and girlfriends. List all the feelings that they identified earlier. But now we also know that parents need relationships, too. So how can this dilemma be solved? Let's brainstorm and see what ideas we can come up with. Have each child suggest a way to cope with this dilemma and why it will work. If they can't come up with a suggestion, then have them pick from the slips of paper (from the **Ways to Cope** handout), read the suggestion that they picked, and explain why it might help.

*Processing* (4 minutes)

10. Sometimes it is difficult to accept that Mom or Dad likes or loves someone other than your father or mother. It takes a while to get used to that idea. Let's everyone go around and finish the sentence: *One thing I could do if I am sad that my Mom or Dad is dating someone else is XXX.*

*Closing* (3 minutes)

11. Play **"I Tried"** and sing along.

# Ways to Cope

Talk with parent

Talk with friend

Talk to an adult (counselor, family member, teacher, family friend)

Write down your feelings

Listen to one of Dan's songs

Talk to a friend who is in the same situation as you

Talk to an adult whose parents are divorced

Ask someone what they would do if they felt the way you do

Brainstorm 10 solutions to your problem

Imagine yourself spilling milk/food/wine on someone, laugh, and then think about how you can express your feelings

# 10-A

# Coping With Blended Families

## GOALS FOR THE SESSION

1. To identify potentially difficult situations with stepparents, stepsiblings, and half siblings.
2. To brainstorm ways to cope with these situations.
3. To practice ways to cope with these situations.

## MATERIALS

- Banner with group name and ground rules hanging on the wall
- "If You Believe In You" tape (specifically the "I Tried" and "I Am A Kid" songs)
- Large notepad and markers
- Coping With Blended Families handout cut into individual slips of paper
- Puppet

## GROUP SESSION

*Warm-Up* (5 minutes)

1. Play **"I Tried"** and sing along (3 minutes).

2. **Working to Be a Family** (2 minutes). Dan is singing about meeting his mother's boyfriend and his father's girlfriend. At the beginning of the song, he sings about spilling milk on his father's girlfriend and spilling wine and food on his mother's boyfriend. At the end of the song, he is singing that he knows he can't get his Mom and Dad back together and that Mike and Rene were OK. When you first meet new people, you need time to get to know them and figure out how to relate to them. If your parents remarry, it takes a while to learn how to be a family. You need to have some happy times together, but there will be some misunderstandings sometimes, too. Today we are going to talk about some of the things that typically happen when people work toward being a family.

*Working Activities* (30 minutes)

3. **Changes and Problems That Happen in Newly Formed Families** (10 minutes). Let's take a few minutes and list some of the changes that happen when parents remarry, have a new partner, or have more children after the divorce. (As a child says something similar to one of the statements on a small piece of paper cut from the handout, put it in the pile. Write any new statements on a piece of paper and add them to the pile.)

4. **Role-Play Practice** (20 minutes). Let's pretend that we are Dear Abby and children are asking us for advice. Let each child pick a puppet. Have each child volunteer to pick a situation from the pile of paper situations and then have their puppet tell Dear Abby the problem. Then have each child using their puppet respond as Dear Abby.

*Processing* (7 minutes)

5. We have been focusing on some of the problems that occur as people learn to be a family. We have come up with some good ideas about ways to cope with these situations. Every situation has problems and also some good things that happen from it. Now let's talk about some of the good stuff that happens as a result of being a part of a blended family. Let's everyone go around and finish the sentence: *One good thing about being in a blended family is XXX.* (If a child can't come up with something good, ask other children to help or you add an answer.)

*Closing* (3 minutes)

6. Sing along to **"I Am A Kid."**

# Coping With Blended Families

My Mom (or Dad) lives in her (or his) new partner's house, so it doesn't feel like my home. I don't like to go over there. What should I do?

What do I call my father's new wife or my mother's new husband?

My Mom (or Dad) asks me all kinds of questions about the other's new partner when I come home from a visit. I don't feel comfortable telling her (or him). What should I do?

I am an only child, and now my Dad (or Mom) has a new baby. I don't get much time alone with them. What can I do?

My Mom (or Dad) has a new partner, and she (or he) has several children who live with them. How am I supposed to get along with them?

My Mom (or Dad) has a new partner, and she (or he) has several children who live with them. The rules for them are different than the rules for me. What do I do?

The rules at my Dad's house are different from the rules at my Mom's house. What do I do?

My new stepmother (or stepfather) punishes me when I do something wrong. I don't think she (or he) should do that.

My Mom (or Dad) likes to spend more time with her (or his) new partner than me.

Other:

Other:

# 10-B

# The Stages of Stepfamilies

**GOALS FOR THE SESSION**

1. To describe the stages that step-families go through.
2. To identify what stages children's families are in.
3. To brainstorm ways to cope with the stage that the family is in.

**MATERIALS**

- Banner with group name and ground rules hanging on the wall
- "If You Believe In You" tape (specifically the "I Am A Kid" song)
- Large notepad and markers
- **Stages of Stepfamilies** worksheet

## GROUP SESSION

*Warm-Up* (5 minutes)

1. Play the **"I Am A Kid"** song and sing along (3 minutes).

2. Today we are going to talk about our new families. It takes a while to develop into a new family, know what the rules are, and figure out how to get along with new parents and new siblings and other relatives (2 minutes).

*Working Activities* (32 minutes)

3. **Stages of Stepfamilies** (15 minutes). Some people have studied stepfamilies and how they become a family and have come up with some stages that families go through. Let's go through each stage and talk about what happens at that point. (Hand out **Stages of Stepfamilies** worksheet for them to follow along.)

**Stage 1: Fantasy.** Characterized by parents' instant expectation of hope and adjustment and children's denial of the situation—they will go away.

**Stage 2: Pseudofamily.** Characterized by vague sense that things are not going well. Family may split along biological lines; parents may be upset with each other over issues around the children. Stepparents with no children may feel left out.

**Stage 3: Awareness.** Characterized by growing awareness of family pressures. Parents feel pulled between

89

needs of biological children and new spouse. Children may observe and exploit differences between the couple.

**Stage 4: Mobilization.** Parents may argue. Parents divided between children. Possibility of a separation.

**Stage 5: Action.** Characterized by couple working together to find solutions. Family structure changes. Children may resist change. Often takes 3 to 4 years to reach this stage.

**Stage 6: Contact.** Characterized by the couple working well together. Stepparents and children get along.

**Stage 7: Resolution.** Characterized by having an identity as a family. Can deal effectively with difficulties.

4. **What Can We Do to Help People Work Together and Feel Connected as a Family at Each Stage?** (17 minutes). Let's go through the worksheet and make suggestions for each stage about what children can do to help make things work.

*Processing* (5 minutes)

5. It takes a while for families to learn how to be a family. Different people have different styles of communicating, loving, and taking care of each other. People need to talk to each other, work out problems, and have good times together to get to be a family. Let's everyone go around and finish this sentence: *One thing that children of divorce can do to help be a part of their new family is XXX because XXX.*

*Closing* (3 minutes)

6. Play **"I Am A Kid"** and sing along.

# Stages of
# Stepfamilies Worksheet

| STAGE | UNREALISTIC EXPECTATIONS | WAYS TO COPE/ GET ALONG |
|---|---|---|
| Fantasy | Parents think the new kids will love me instantly.<br>The kids ignore the new parent, hoping they will go away. | |
| Pseudofamily | Of course, we get along perfectly.<br>There are no problems forming a family. | |
| Awareness | The other children/parent are the problem. | |
| Mobilization | There is a right way to do things. | |
| Action | It is too hard to work this out. | |
| Contact | It is too hard to work this out. | |
| Resolution | There will never be any problems. | |

# 4

# Closing Sessions

- **Achieving closure.**
- **Tasks of the termination stage.**
- **Processing termination.**

Closure is an essential part of any small-group experience and is particularly important for psychoeducational groups and young children. Many prominent group workers suggest that one must always allow two to four sessions for ending groups (Gazda, 1989; Maples, 1988). However, pragmatically, with a short-term group such as a six- to eight-session children of divorce group, one complete session on termination is probably most realistic.

Separation, closure, and feelings and fear of abandonment are often issues for children of divorce. Children of divorce may be experiencing any or all of these events as a result of the divorce. They may be separated from someone they love and depend on, they may have been abandoned (or perceive themselves as abandoned), and/or they may not have had the opportunity to say good-bye to important people in their lives. Thus, it is essential to deal effectively with the termination of the children of divorce group.

Several suggestions are given to do this. First, the number of sessions for a children of divorce group should be established before the group begins, and the children (and parents) should be informed of it from the beginning of the selection process. It is helpful to put the number of sessions (and an ending date) in writing for both parents and children as part of the information about the group as well as the consent form.

In addition, it is important to announce when the group is half over and that there are only so many sessions left at the midpoint of the group. After doing so, it is important to give the children time to reflect on the eventual ending of the group. They may not have much of a reaction at first, but sometimes they will experience feelings about the group being over or the leader "leaving them." Such events are "teachable moments" in groups, with the leader being able to help the members discuss their feelings and then problem solve and plan for the future. Yes, the group is over, but what can you take from it? No, we won't meet anymore, but who from this group can you talk to about your family? Who else in your life listens to you like the members of this group? What have you learned from this group that you can continue to do after group ends?

It is also very useful to remind members of a children of divorce group that there is only one session left as they leave the second-to-last session and to ask them to think about what they have learned, what has been helpful in the group, and how each member has helped them. Written activities at this time are particularly useful so that children are prepared to discuss the ending of the group and how they have benefited from the group; otherwise, children may not think about the group or what they have been asked to think about again until they arrive at the last session.

There are several tasks during the termination stage of a group. Jacobs et al. (1988) described them as follows: reviewing and summarizing the group experience, assessing members' growth and change, finishing business, applying change to everyday life, providing feedback, handling good-byes, and planning for continued problem resolution (p. 259). Although these seven tasks may seem to be a lot for one session of a children of divorce group for elementary school students, many of the tasks overlap and can be performed within a short time frame. With a little planning and some homework assigned the week before, one session can accomplish most, if not all, of the goals recommended by Jacobs et al. A series of questions to structure the last session, even for elementary school students, will focus the children on the important tasks of summarizing what has happened in group, what they have learned, and what they can continue to do after group has ended. For example, the following questions focus on summarizing the group, applying change to everyday life, and planning for continued problem resolution: What have you learned about yourself from this group? What have you learned about children of divorce in general? What have we done in this group that is important for all children of divorce to do? What would they learn from it? What have you learned from the songs? What have you learned that you can continue to do after group? What songs can you listen to to remind you of specific coping techniques? When will you listen to them? What will they remind you to do?

The following questions focus on assessing members' change and providing feedback: How are you different from when you started this group? What situations would you handle differently? What would you do differently? What would all children of divorce learn from being in this group? How would they be different? What would Kelly and Cory learn from this group? How would they feel at the end of this group? Who in this group has been helpful and how? Who in this group has said something that you connected with and what was it? Thank other members for what they have shared with you about being children of divorce (be specific).

Three examples of closing sessions follow. Each of the sessions can be used independently as a last session or can be sequenced to end a children of divorce group.

# E-A

# Ending

## Sidebar

**GOALS FOR THE SESSION**

1. To identify what each child has learned from the group.
2. To identify strategies to cope with the divorce and tough situations.

**MATERIALS**

- Banner with group name and ground rules hanging on the wall
- "If You Believe In You" tape (specifically the "And I Need A Lot Of Love" and "So Am I" songs)
- Large notepad and markers
- Drawing paper and crayons and markers

## GROUP SESSION

*Review* (8 minutes)

1. Sing the **"And I Need A Lot Of Love"** song (3 minutes).

2. **Which Song Is Most Helpful for Children of Divorce?** (5 minutes). Everyone takes a turn and states: *The song on Dan's tape that helps kids with divorce the most is XXX because XXX.*

*Working Activities* (26 minutes)

3. **Important Lessons About Divorce, Families, and Feelings** (14 minutes). Today is the last time that this group will meet, and so it is important to talk about what you have learned about divorce, your families, and your feelings. So each one of us is going to write and/or draw what is most important for kids to know about divorce, families, and feelings. Each of us can probably come up with several ideas about what is important, so let's get started. (Pass out paper and crayons and markers.)

4. Let's everyone go around and share what it is important to know about divorce, families, and feelings. If someone says something good that you didn't write down, you can add it to your list as we go around (12 minutes).

5. As leader, write down on a sheet of paper each of the messages the children mention.

*Processing* (8 minutes)

6. **Important Themes in Songs.** Using the list of important messages, identify which song or songs from Dan's tape help get that message across. Encourage children to add the names of the songs to their sheets.

*Closing* (3 minutes)

7. Sing the **"So Am I"** song.

*Homework*

8. Tell the children to take home their drawing and hang it where they can look at it when they need to.

# E-B

# What Have I Learned From This Group?

## GROUP SESSION

*Review* (8 minutes)

1. **Review of Topics.** Today is the last week that our group is going to meet. So we are going to spend time today finishing things up, talking about what we have learned, how we are different as a result of this group, and how we got that way. We have been meeting for XX weeks now, and we have talked about a lot of different things. Let's go through and just quickly list all the different things we have talked about in here. I'll write them down on this large notepad.

   That's a great list. Let's hang it up as a reminder for us as we finish our session today.

*Working Activities* (28 minutes)

2. **What Have We Learned From This Group?** (9 minutes). Pass out a small piece of paper to each child. Ask them to write down on the piece of paper the most important thing that they have learned from this group. Have the children pass the papers to you, and you mix them up. Then give one member (or your coleader) an $8^{1}/_{2}$ by 11-inch piece of paper and a marker. Tell them that you are going to read off anonymously what people have learned and that the person with the paper will then write down what has been learned. Each member will get a copy of the paper to take home.

3. **How Did This Group Help?** (9 minutes). Pass out a small piece of paper to each child. Ask them to write down on the piece of paper the most important thing that they did in this group to help them feel better about the divorce. Have the children pass the papers to you, and you mix them up. Then give one member (or your coleader) an $8\frac{1}{2}$ by 11-inch piece of paper and a marker. Tell them that you are going to read off anonymously what has helped people feel better and that the person with the paper will then write down what has helped. Each member will get a copy of the paper to take home.

4. **What Did Each Member Contribute to the Group?** (10 minutes). Explain that it is the members of each group that make a group successful and that they all have worked very hard to make this group a good group, a safe group, and a group in which they can share feelings and thoughts. It is important that each member knows how they have helped others because we each tend to underestimate how much we help others. Pass out the pieces of paper with each member's name on it and the words "You helped me when you . . . ." Do not give them to the person whose name is at the top. Explain that each person will write, anonymously, a statement about when the other person helped them. Give them about 1 minute for each person, then have them switch—keep passing them until everyone has written on everyone else's paper.

*Processing* (6 minutes)

5. What do you think that I did as a leader that I should do if I lead another group for children of divorce? What topics should be covered? What activities were helpful? What songs were relevant? What should I do? What shouldn't I do?

*Closing* (3 minutes)

6. Play the **"Everybody Needs A Friend"** song.

7. Give them copies of the lists from Numbers 2 and 3. Make sure that they take home their paper from Number 4.

# E-C

# What Can
# I Do Differently?

**GOALS FOR
THE SESSION**

1. To identify what
each child has
learned from the
group.
2. To identify
potentially diffi-
cult situations
and strategies to
cope with them.

**MATERIALS**

- Banner with group
name and ground
rules hanging on
the wall
- "If You Believe In
You" tape
- Large notepad and
markers
- Paper and crayons
and markers
- Handout titled
**Letter to Dan and
Kelly and Cory**

## GROUP SESSION

*Review* (13 minutes)

1. **Decide on a Theme Song for Our Group** (10 minutes). We picked a group name at the beginning of
this group, but we didn't pick a theme song. Theme
songs usually reflect something important about the
group. We have used songs throughout the group, so
it makes sense that we should have a song to remember the group by and maybe remind us of the things
that we learned from this group. Which song should
be our theme song? Have each child state at least
one theme song for the group and why they think
that this song reflects their group and its goals. Then
discuss which song they like. If necessary, have them
vote on a song. Add the theme song to the banner
on the wall.

2. **Play the theme song and sing along** (3 minutes).

*Working Activities* (25 minutes)

3. **A Letter to Dan to Summarize What They Have
Learned From This Group** (15 minutes). Dan and
Kelly and Cory seemed to be a big part of this group
in some ways. A lot of times through their songs they
shared what happened for them, and then we talked
about what happened for us. It is important as this
group ends to summarize and remind ourselves what
we have learned and what might be helpful to other
children of divorce. So let's each write a letter to

Dan and Kelly and Cory that tells them how this group has been helpful. Then I'll read each one out loud. Hand out the outline for the letter. Read through it aloud and help the children to fill in the blanks.

4.  Collect the letters, shuffle them, and read each aloud. Tell them that you will be sending them to Dan and Kelly and Cory so that they know how their music affected the group (10 minutes).

*Processing* (4 minutes)

5.  **Processing of Reactions to Letters.** Let's talk for a minute about the letters we just read. Everyone's letter was a little different. What did you hear in someone else's letter that you think is really important that Dan, Kelly, and Cory hear? What else should we let them know?

*Closing* (3 minutes)

6.  **Ending.** Let's get in a circle and hold hands and sing our theme song. Play the song again.

# Letter to
# Dan and Kelly and Cory

DEAR DAN, KELLY, AND CORY,

THANK YOU FOR SINGING YOUR SONGS AND SHARING YOUR EXPERIENCES OF DIVORCE WITH US. I LIKED THE _____ SONG THE BEST BECAUSE IT HELPED CHILDREN OF DIVORCE LEARN THAT _____

_____

_____

IN OUR CHILDREN OF DIVORCE GROUP, WE TALKED ABOUT:

1.
2.
3.

WE ALSO LEARNED SEVERAL NEW THINGS THAT MAY HELP WHEN WE ARE ANGRY, SAD, OR UPSET ABOUT THE DIVORCE:

1.
2.
3.

_____

_____

_____

_____

THANKS!!!

# 5

# Adaptations of This Manual

- Junior high school students
- High school students
- Culturally diverse groups
- Other psychoeducational and counseling groups
- Classroom guidance activities
- Parent groups
- Individual counseling
- Adult discussions with a child

This manual was written specifically for elementary school age children, but it has a multitude of adaptations. It can be easily adapted to junior high school students with some minor wording changes and slight variations in the activities. High school students enjoy planning group activities using the songs for younger children. Such an activity enables older students to examine and talk about their issues and experiences related to being children of divorce within the context of helping younger children. It is the author's experience that high school students enjoy the altruistic value of creating something for someone else as well as being able to revisit their experiences and how they coped with the divorce in positive, healthy ways. Multicultural adaptations are possible as well with the framework of this group. Many of the songs are applicable to other psychoeducational and counseling groups in schools and classroom guidance activities. The material may even be adapted to a parents' divorce group. In addition, the material may be adapted outside of a group with one counselor working with one child or an adult discussing the divorce with a son or daughter. This chapter suggests ways to make these adaptations.

## JUNIOR HIGH SCHOOL STUDENTS

Much of this manual as written can be used with junior high school students. They may need less time to brainstorm ideas and ways to cope; more time may be spent on role-playing and practicing new ways of behaving. These students have a little more control over their environment than do elementary school students, and so more alternatives to current situations are possible. Furthermore, issues such as freedom, independence, and balancing two families and a social life may dominate sessions. At this time in their lives, they are often rebelling against authority, and that greatly influences relationships with their parents, stepparents, and potential stepparents.

Junior high school students, although at first they may protest, often enjoy the music as much as their younger counterparts. Sessions that are particularly productive are those that allow the students to write their own songs or verses to the songs that tap into the students' creativity and feelings as well as acknowledge that they are not little kids.

## HIGH SCHOOL STUDENTS

High school students will acknowledge that the songs are cute but, particularly if the divorce occurred several years ago, often say that they are used to it and have resolved all the issues around it. It's not a problem anymore. One way to encourage children of divorce to continue to examine their difficulties with the divorce and the new circumstances (especially if others are suggesting that they are still having difficulty with the divorce) is to frame the group as an altruistic activity. Advertise the group as a community service project designed to help elementary school children cope with divorce. Ideally a group of 6 to 10 students (or subgroups of 6) can design one of the following using the songs: (a) a 3- or 4-week group to help children of divorce begin to talk about their feelings about the divorce, (b) a play that helps children of divorce begin to think about the issues that they must deal with as the divorce proceeds, or (c) a presentation that discusses key issues for children of divorce. To do this, the high school students must think about their experiences, critical issues, important themes that have been helpful to them in dealing with the divorce, and words of wisdom for the younger children. The group counselor can function as a facilitator, keeping the group on task, asking questions to identify key issues and explore current feelings about the divorce, coordinating the group meetings, and arranging for the presentation at a local elementary school.

## CULTURALLY DIVERSE GROUPS

The music to be used with this manual, although it appeals to a wide audience, could be characterized as a little folksy. Children today listen to very different kinds of music and so may react to the songs with comments like "that's not our kind of music." This may especially be an issue in racially diverse groups or areas. Students may be listening to rap, hip-hop, or heavy metal and may not identify with this kind of music. That's OK. What is important is that the students listen to the words and hear the message. One of the goals of using music is to enhance the students' creativity and to help them get in touch with affect in different kinds of ways. Writing their own songs or verses to a song is a creative way to deal with different tastes in music and to encourage students to put their individual stories to music. Students may want to adapt a song to a different beat, for example, try **"Divorce"** as a rap song or **"Bad Mood"** in hip-hop. It is helpful to introduce the songs as Dan's and Kelly's and Cory's way of expressing themselves and then suggest that they express themselves musically as well. It is also helpful to ask students to bring in songs that affect them emotionally or to say something about their experience of divorce, again translating their story into music.

## OTHER PSYCHOEDUCATIONAL AND COUNSELING GROUPS

Much of the content of the sessions as well as specific songs could be used in other psychoeducational and counseling groups in elementary schools. Communication skills, self-esteem, anger management, and general counseling groups could all incorporate aspects of the sessions. General sessions such as Introduction to Each Other and to the Group, How Our Group Can Work Together, What Are Our Families Like?, Our Families and Friends: Who Can We Talk To?, Communication Skills, Nonverbal Communication, Life Is Tough and Some Ways to Cope With It, Different Types of Families, Ending, What Have I Learned From This Group?, and What Can I Do Differently? could all be easily adapted to other types of groups. Other sessions such as Worries, Worries About the Divorce and Who Is Responsible for Them, Feelings About the Divorce, Sad Feelings About the Divorce or Separation, Feeling Angry About the Divorce, and New Traditions could all be adapted to other types of groups simply by shifting the focus from the divorce to the skills being taught in that session and changing the role-play situations.

All of the songs on the **"If You Believe In You"** tape are focused on self-esteem and good communication and, thus, could be used in a variety of psychoeducational and counseling groups. **"And I Need A Lot Of Love"** and **"I Am A Kid"** focus on the special needs and the uniqueness of children and could easily be incorporated into self-esteem groups. **"Perfect People"** focuses on the desire to be perfect and how hard it is to make mistakes in front of others; it is helpful to ask children to listen to the song and then talk about times when they have tried to be perfect and what happened. **"Casey The Clown"** could be used in groups to highlight how students who are having trouble at home may be acting out at school and how a school counselor can be helpful to such students. **"Bad Mood"** is a great song to use in self-esteem groups or groups that focus on social skills, communication, or anger management; it reinforces the idea that everyone is in a bad mood sometimes, but you still need to be polite to people. **"So Am I"** emphasizes that everyone has tough situations to deal with and that all people, even kids, have strength and ways to cope with the tough stuff.

"**Everybody Needs A Friend**" reinforces the importance of talking to someone about your troubles, whereas "**If You Believe In You**" stresses the importance of feeling good about and believing in yourself. "**I Worry**" can be used to help children to identify what kinds of things they worry about and who can help them with their worries. "**Is It My Fault?**" can help children to dispel some magical thinking (that is developmental) by asking them to look at how they often may think that something is their fault when it really is not.

## CLASSROOM GUIDANCE ACTIVITIES

Because many of the songs and activities are focused on imparting information and skill building, they may also be used in classroom guidance activities. Self-esteem, communication skills, healthy families, and friendship skills are all topics that school counselors are often asked to present as a classroom activity. Sessions such as What Are Our Families Like?, Our Families and Friends: Who Can We Talk To? Communication Skills, Nonverbal Communication, and Different Types of Families could be used as independent classroom guidance activities. With minor modifications, the following sessions could also be conducted in classrooms: Feelings About the Divorce (to Feelings in General), Life Is Tough and Some Ways to Cope With It, and New Traditions.

## PARENT GROUPS

The goal of children of divorce groups is to help the children cope more adaptively with a potentially difficult situation, parental divorce. Many recommended activities suggest that children express their feelings and talk directly with their parents about what is happening. A group for parents helps parents to gain a sense of what their children are learning in a children of divorce group and learn some strategies to deal with some of the potential changes in their children's behavior and ways to handle situations that are particularly difficult (Beech Acres Aring Institute, 1993).

In recent years, courts have often mandated that parents involved in divorces with children under the age of 18 attend a workshop focused on how to help the children adjust to the divorce and/or how to be effective coparents in the future. As a matter of pragmatism, children may be able to attend a workshop at the same time focused on their needs around the divorce instead of just going to day care while their parents attend the workshop. However it happens, it makes sense that parents and children participate in a psychoeducational group simultaneously so that both are learning new skills to adjust to the divorce. Topics that are useful in parental groups include how to help your children express their feelings about the divorce; how to discuss the divorce with them; what information children need to know and what information children don't need to know; how to keep the children out of the middle of the divorce, custody, and visitation issues; how to discuss dating and remarriage with children; and typical problem situations, reactions, and ways to intervene.

It is recommended that parents' groups parallel the children of divorce groups, using the same topics and music each week as the children do. This enables the parents (a) to know what the children have been discussing and be prepared to continue the discussion with their children and (b) to explore their thoughts, feelings, and behavior about key issues related to children of divorce in preparation for (a).

## INDIVIDUAL COUNSELING

Much of the group sessions can be adapted for a counselor working one-on-one with a child in individual counseling. Although it may not be necessary to spend an extensive amount of time on ground rules and naming the group, the content of the introductory sessions can be useful to the child. The songs can be used to help children universalize and normalize the experience of having parents who have divorced and to help them think about other people (peers and adults) who have been in similar circumstances and would understand if they talked with them about their experiences. The content sessions can be chosen on the basis of what issues the particular child is currently struggling with. The procedures would be similar to the group outline in that the song(s) can be played and then the child can be asked the questions or engage in the activities in conjunction with the counselor. The counselor may be able to continually normalize and universalize the experience for the individual child by adding comments such as "When I work with a group of children of divorce, they often report . . . or say . . . or feel . . . XXX." Two sessions may be able to be combined because the length of activities may be shortened when only one child is participating.

## ADULT DISCUSSIONS WITH A CHILD

A concerned adult (parent, relative, or friend) may also be able to use the activities suggested in this manual individually with a child. Similar guidelines apply as when a counselor is working with a child. The most important guideline when the adult is not trained as a counselor is that the adult should have some understanding of the common issues children of divorce experience and potential therapeutic interventions. The focus should be on encouraging the expression of feelings by the child as well as normalizing the experience and making universal statements. Resources suggested in Appendix G could be read in preparation for such discussions with a child. Particularly useful would be books such as *Good Answers to Tough Questions About Divorce* (Berry, 1990), *The Parents' Book About Divorce* (Gardner, 1991), and *Growing Up With Divorce: Helping Your Child Avoid Immediate and Later Emotional Problems* (Kalter, 1990).

## DISCUSSION AND CONCLUSIONS

Parental divorce is a significant issue for children of divorce. It is a lifelong issue and one where psychoeducational and counseling interventions may benefit children at various points in their school career and in their lives. It is essential that counselors be prepared to work with children of divorce both individually and in groups. Groups provide elements of support, altruism, universality, and cooperation that individual counseling cannot provide. Creative arts are an important component of any intervention with children. Creative arts such as puppetry, drawing, and music are particularly important to help children of divorce express their feelings related to the divorce and practice new behaviors and skills in a safe and supportive environment.

# References

Amato, P. R., & Keith, B. (1991). Parental divorce and the well-being of children: A meta-analysis. *Psychological Bulletin, 110*, 26–46.

Barker, J., Brinkman, L., & Deardoff, M. (1995). Computer interventions for adolescent children of divorce. *Journal of Divorce and Remarriage, 23*, 197–213.

Beech Acres Aring Institute. (1993). *The boys and girls group: Divorce and stepfamilies* (4th ed.). Cincinnati, OH: Author.

Berry, J. (1990). *Good answers to tough questions about divorce.* San Francisco: Children's Press.

Bloch, S., Reibstein, J., Crouch, E., Holroyd, P., & Themen, J. (1979). A method for study of therapeutic factors in group psychotherapy. *British Journal of Psychiatry, 134*, 257–263.

Bornstein, M. T., Bornstein, P. H., & Walters, H. A. (1988). Children of divorce: Empirical evaluation of a group-treatment program. *Journal of Clinical Child Psychology, 17*, 248–254.

Cantrell, R. G. (1986). Adjustment to divorce: Three components to assist children. *Elementary School Guidance & Counseling, 20*, 163–173.

Cebollero, A. M., Cruise, K., & Stollak, G. (1987). The long-term effects of divorce: Mothers and children in concurrent support groups. *Journal of Divorce, 10*, 219–228.

Conley, D. (1994). *If you believe in you* [Cassette]. New York: Treehouse Music.

Crosbie-Burnett, M., & Newcomer, L. L. (1990). Group counseling children of divorce: The effects of a multimodal intervention. *Journal of Divorce, 13*, 69–78.

DeLucia-Waack, J. L. (1996). Children of divorce group work in the schools. In S. T. Gladding (Ed.), *New developments in group counseling* (pp. 27–28). Greensboro, NC: ERIC/CASS.

DeLucia-Waack, J. L. (2000). *Treatment manual for using music in children of divorce groups.* Available from author.

Gardner, R. (1991). *The parents' book about divorce.* New York: Bantam Books.

Garvin, V., Leber, D., & Kalter, N. (1991). Children of divorce: Predictors of change following preventive intervention. *American Journal of Orthopsychiatry, 61*, 438–447.

Gazda, G. M. (1989). *Group counseling: A developmental approach* (4th ed.). Boston: Allyn & Bacon.

Gladding, S. T. (1991). *Group work: A counseling specialty.* New York: Macmillan.

Gladding, S. T. (1998). *Counseling as an art: The creative arts in counseling* (2nd ed.). Alexandria, VA: American Counseling Association.

Guldner, C. A., & O'Connor, T. (1991). The ALF Group: A model of group therapy with children. *Journal of Group Psychotherapy, 43*, 184–190.

Gwynn, C. A., & Brantley, H. T. (1987). Effects of a divorce group intervention for elementary school children. *Psychology in the Schools, 24*, 161–164.

Harter, S. (1982). The Perceived Competence Scale for Children. *Child Development, 53*, 87–97.

Howard, S. S., & Scherman, A. (1990). *An evaluation of an educational group for children of divorced families.* City, OK: Publisher. (ERIC Document Reproduction Services No. ED 320 068)

Jacobs, E. E., Harvill, R. L., & Masson, R. L. (1988). *Group counseling: Strategies and skills.* Pacific Grove, CA: Brooks/Cole.

Kalter, N. (1990). *Growing up with divorce: Helping your child avoid immediate and later emotional problems.* New York: Free Press.

Kalter, N. (1998). Group interventions for children of divorce. In K. C. Stoiber & T. R. Kratochwill (Eds.), *Handbook of group intervention for children and families* (pp. 120–140). Boston: Allyn & Bacon.

Kivlighan, D. M., Jr., & Goldfine, D. C. (1991). Endorsement of therapeutic factors as a function of stage of group development and participant interpersonal attitudes. *Journal of Counseling Psychology, 38,* 150–158.

Kovacs, M. (1981). Rating scales to assess depression in school-aged children. *Acta Paedopsychiatrica, 46,* 305–315.

Kovacs, M. (1992). *The Children's Depression Inventory manual.* North Tonawanda, NY: Multi-Health Systems.

Kurdek, L., & Berg, B. (1987). Children's Beliefs About Parental Divorce Scale: Psychometric characteristics and concurrent validity. *Journal of Consulting and Clinical Psychology, 55,* 712–718.

Maples, M. F. (1988). Group development: Extending Tuckman's theory. *Journal for Specialists in Group Work, 13,* 17–23.

Morganett, R. S. (1990). *Skills for living: Group counseling for young adolescents.* Champaign, IL: Research Press.

Mulholland, D. J., Watt, N. F., Philpott, A., & Sarlin, N. (1991). Academic performance in children of divorce: Psychological resilience and vulnerability. *Psychiatry, 54,* 268–280.

Nelson, R. E., & Crawford, B. (1990). Suicide among elementary school children. *Elementary School Guidance & Counseling, 25,* 123–128.

Pfeiffer, W., & Jones, J. (1975). Co-facilitating. In W. Pfeiffer & J. Jones (Eds.), *A handbook of structured experiences for human relations training* (Vols. 1–5, pp. 219–222). La Jolla, CA: University Associates.

Reynolds, C. R., & Richmond, B. O. (1985). *Revised Children's Manifest Anxiety Scale.* Los Angeles: Western Psychological Services.

Ritchie, M., & Huss, S. (2000). Recruitment and screening of minors for group counseling. *Journal for Specialists in Group Work, 25,* 146–156.

Rosenstein-Manner, M. (1990). *An evaluation of school-based support groups for children of divorced or separated parents* (Report No. 195). City, Ontario, Canada: Publisher. (ERIC Document Reproduction Service No. ED 328 836)

Spigelman, A., & Spigelman, G. (1991). Indications of depression and distress in divorce and nondivorce children reflected by the Rorschach test. *Journal of Personality Assessment, 57,* 120–129.

Wilcoxon, S. A., & Magnusom, S. (1999). Considerations for school counselors serving noncustodial parents: Premises and suggestions. *Professional School Counseling, 2,* 275–279.

Yalom, I. D. (1995). *The theory and practice of group psychotherapy* (4th ed.). New York: Basic Books.

Yauman, B. E. (1991). School-based group counseling for children of divorce: A review of the literature. *Elementary School Guidance & Counseling, 26,* 130–138.

## WORDS TO
## "IF YOU BELIEVE IN YOU"
## SONGS

# List of Songs by Session

| SONG | SESSION TITLE |
| --- | --- |
| "Divorce" | Introduction to Each Other and to the Group |
| | Lots of Children Have Parents Who Are Divorced |
| | How Our Group Can Work Together |
| | How Divorce Happened in My Family |
| | What Do All the Big Words Mean for Me? |
| | Feelings About the Divorce |
| | Feeling Angry About the Divorce |
| | The Emotional Process of Divorce |
| "Everybody Needs A Friend" | How Our Group Can Work Together |
| | Our Families and Friends: Who Can We Talk To? |
| | Worries |
| | Worries About the Divorce and Who Is Responsible for Them |
| | Feelings About the Divorce |
| | Communication Skills |
| | What Have I Learned From this Group? |
| | New People in Our Lives |
| | Sad Feelings About the Divorce or Separation |
| "So Am I" | How Divorce Happened in My Family |
| | What Are Our Families Like? |
| | Worries About the Divorce and Who Is Responsible for Them |
| | Life Is Tough and Some Ways to Cope With It |
| | Ending |
| | The Emotional Process of Divorce |
| | How to Cope With Parental Fighting |
| "I Worry" | Worries |
| | Worries About the Divorce and Who Is Responsible for Them |
| | Sad Feelings About the Divorce or Separation |
| "And I Need A Lot Of Love" | Is It My Fault? |
| | Different Types of Families |
| | Visitation |
| | Ending |
| | Maintaining Parental Relationships |
| "Is It My Fault?" | Is It My Fault? |

| SONG | SESSION TITLE |
| --- | --- |
| **"I Tried"** | I Tried to Get My Mom and Dad Back Together Again<br>Still Trying to Get My Mom and Dad Back Together Again<br>My Mom and Dad Are Dating Other People?<br>New People in Our Lives<br>Coping With Blended Families |
| **"Bad Mood"** | Some Ways to Cope With Parents Who Don't Live Together<br>How to Cope With Parental Fighting<br>Maintaining Parental Relationships |
| **"Casey The Clown"** | Communication Skills |
| **"I Am A Kid"** | New Traditions<br>Coping With Blended Families<br>The Stages of Stepfamilies |

# "And I Need A Lot Of Love"

A flower needs sunshine, good soil, and some rain
You may remember a scarecrow who needed a brain
A school bus needs yellow, a pine tree needs green
An artist needs the courage to see what's never been seen

> But I'm just a kid and I need a lot
> I'm just a kid and I need a lot
> I'm just a kid and I need a lot of love

A monkey needs a jungle, to swing wild and free
A poet needs a lonely night like a sailor needs a sea
And all of these feelings
Need somewhere to go
The way an eagle needs to fly and a river needs to flow

> But I'm just a kid and I need a lot
> I'm just a kid and I need a lot
> I'm just a kid and I need a lot of love

I open my window wide
I gaze at the world outside
I wave my arms and say hello
I've got so much to give
I want to live live live
And I need you to help me grow

A star needs the twilight
A day needs the dawn
An old heart needs new hope
Like a singer needs a song
A rainbow, a beanbag
A tiger and a flea
For some mysterious reason
These things need to be

> But I'm just a kid and I need a lot
> I'm just a kid and I need a lot
> I'm just a kid and I need a lot of love

# "Divorce"

My Mom and Dad could not get along
A good thing went bad that's why I'm singing about this song
It's a song about darkness, a song about light
It's a song about the way things go when they don't go right

I remember the morning . . . it was a rainy day
They woke me up, sat me down, said they had something serious to say
At first I was shocked, I could not believe
One was gonna stay and the other was gonna leave

> Divorce, everybody's heard of divorce
> A hurting little word divorce
> So rough and so real
> I hope you understand the way I feel

It happened to Ashley, it happened to Sue
It happened to Jamie, Joey and Amy
And now it's happened to me too
Sometimes I feel angry, sometimes I feel sad
But when I talk about it then it doesn't seem to hurt so bad

> Divorce, everybody's heard of divorce
> A hurting little word divorce
> So rough and so real
> I hope you understand the way I feel

I still believe in sunny days
Not a cloud in the sky
Not a tear in my eye
Gonna wipe that tear out of my eye

Some day when I grow up I'm gonna find a wife
And when we get married I hope we stay married for life
Just so our kids won't have to go through
All of this stuff I've been singing about for you

> Divorce, everybody's heard of divorce
> A hurting little word divorce
> So rough and so real
> I hope you understand the way I feel

# "I Tried"

Well since the day they sat me down to say that they were breaking up
I've been walking round moping hoping thinking making up
ways that I could get them back together again

'Cause there's a feeling deep inside of me that wants it like it used to be
to see them acting happily married for eternity for it to be
it's up to me to get them back to acting like friends

> Well I tried, yes I tried
> And I been trying since it all began
> Well I tried, yes I tried
> I been trying again and again
> Yes I tried and I tried
> It's so hard to see it end
> I been trying to get my Mom and Dad back together again.

Well it happened on a Saturday I think it was a cloudy day my Dad said hey
I gotta say I gotta friend her name's Rene she looked at me I looked away
and then I spilled my milk on her dress (it was an accident)

And then one night another time my Mom said here's a friend of mine his name is
Mike
you'll like him fine just give him a little time I bumped into his glass of wine liquid
spilled and food went flying what a mess

> Well I tried, yes I tried
> And I been trying since it all began
> Well I tried, yes I tried
> I been trying again and again
> Yes I tried and I tried
> It's so hard to see it end
> I been trying to get my Mom and Dad back together again.

One day in May it dawned on me that we were never gonna be a great big happy family
The way I wished that it could be and so I said good bye to dreams of happy ever after
Scenes I finally let go

The sun keeps going up and down the world keeps spinning round and round my ship
sunk but I didn't drown eventually I swam aground I cleared my head and finally
found a little boat I learned how to row

# "Is It My Fault?"

I try so hard to be good and do all the things I should
Did I do something bad to make you so mad?
Lately everybody seems so sad

| | |
|---|---|
| Mommy, is it my fault? | It isn't your fault |
| Daddy, is it my fault? | It isn't your fault |
| It feels like my fault | No, it isn't your fault |
| so it must be my fault | No, it isn't your fault |
| Mommy, is it my fault? | No, it isn't your fault |
| Daddy, is it my fault? | No, it isn't your fault |
| I want to hear you say that | |
| it's not my fault | |

Sometimes my room is a mess and I don't always do my best
I'll try real hard to change, my room I'll rearrange
if you'll both stop acting so strange

| | |
|---|---|
| Mommy, is it my fault? | It isn't your fault |
| Daddy, is it my fault? | No, it isn't your fault |
| It feels like my fault | No, it isn't your fault |
| so it must be my fault | No, it isn't your fault |
| Mommy, is it my fault? | No, it isn't your fault |
| Daddy, is it my fault? | No, it isn't your fault |
| Why do I feel this way? | |

| | |
|---|---|
| I want to hear you say | |
| it's not my fault | No, it isn't your fault |
| it's not my fault | No, it isn't your fault |
| I want to hear you say | No, it isn't your fault |
| it's not my fault | No, it isn't your fault |

Why do I feel this way, why do I feel this way, if it's not my fault not my fault my fault
  my fault

When parents get divorced, it's never because of what a kid did it's not your fault

# "Perfect People"

Perfect people are perfectly neat
They never wiggle or squirm in their seat
Their papers are perfectly complete
No runny noses, no smelly feet

    Oh no, not me, I'm not perfect and I never will be
    Oh no, not I, I'll be unperfect 'till the day I die
    Oh no, I'm not one of those perfect people

Perfect people sit perfectly straight
They never hurry, they always wait
They eat every last little green thing on their plate
Don't you think they're just great?

    Oh no, not me, I'm not perfect and I never will be
    Oh no, not I, I'll be unperfect 'till the day I die
    Oh no, I'm not one of those perfect people

Now there's a funny thing about perfect people
I think you'll agree once you listen to this
The funny thing about perfect people
Is that, perfect people don't exist

Perfect people perfect perfect people
Perfect people
Perfect perfect people

# "Casey The Clown"

*Hey did you hear about Casey?*
*Oh boy, what now?*
*I heard he's in the principal's office*
*Wow, do you think he's getting yelled at?*
*Yelled at, Mr. Conley must be ready to kill him by now*
*Well I wish I knew what was going on in there*
*Me too*

Your teacher tells me Casey you been doing lots of cutting up
Little jokes and bumps and pokes and now
She finally got fed up she sent you here hoping maybe I could try and shape
   you up

But Casey what am I to do
With someone who's a clown like you
I swear before your stay is through
You'll make a circus of this school

Casey the Clown, Casey the Clown
Who do you think you're fooling when you're fooling around
We're gonna smile when you lay your clown suit down
Casey Casey Casey Casey the Clown

*Hey, it's been over ½ hour. Do you think he's still alive? I doubt it.*

I've been hearing lately things at home are going rather bad
I know it's hard when things go wrong between somebody's Mom and Dad
And I also know that acting silly can be a disguise for feeling sad

Casey Casey Casey Casey the Clown
Who do you think you're fooling when you're fooling around
We're gonna smile when you lay your clown suit down
Casey Casey Casey Casey the Clown

If there's anything that I can do
To help you cope and make it through
And here's something you never knew
I used to be a clown like you

Casey the Clown, Casey the Clown
Who do you think you're fooling when you're fooling around

We're gonna smile when you lay your clown suit down
Casey Casey Casey Casey the Clown

*Look, here he comes, Hi Casey!*
*Did you see that? He walked right by us. It looked like he had tears in his eyes.*
*Wow, I've never seen Casey cry before, Mr. Conley must have been pretty rough*

# "I Am A Kid"

I am a kid let's get that right
I'm red I'm yellow I'm black I'm white
On a sunny day or stormy night
I'm gonna be OK gonna be all right

    I am a kid, I am a kid,
    I am a kid.
    I'm a K-I K-I KID a KID that's me

I am a kid let's get that straight
I'm seven I'm eleven I'm five I'm eight
They say I've gotta grow up but I can wait
I love love but I hate hate

    I am a kid, I am a kid,
    I am a kid.
    I'm a K-I K-I KID a KID that's me

I am a kid just wanna say hi
Life is tough but so am I
And even on that stormy day
Gonna be OK

    I am a kid, I am a kid,
    I am a kid.
    I'm a K-I K-I KID a KID that's me

I'm just a kid trying to have some fun
Without hurting anyone
And so 'till this song is sung
I am a K-I-D

    I am a kid, I am a kid,
    I am a kid.
    I'm a K-I K-I KID a KID that's me

Come on along and be a kid with me
Every kid has got a right to be
It's time for kids to make some history
Everybody let your kid be free

# "I Worry"

Sometimes I worry about my Mother
Sometimes I worry about my Dad
I worry about who's happy and I worry about who's sad
I worry about my brother after all he's only three
And then there are times, sometimes, when I worry about me

    Who's gonna be there when I'm sad and I need a clown
    Who's gonna give my ice cream cone a lick around
    Who's gonna help me when my problems pile too high
    Who's gonna see when I laugh
    Who's gonna come when I cry

I was talking to my Mother
I was talking to my Dad
They said they'd always be there even when things get bad
And they told me not to worry, but sometimes I still do
And then they said hey, we want you to know we will always love you

    Who's gonna be there when I'm sad and I need a clown
    Who's gonna give my ice cream cone a lick around
    Who's gonna help me when my problems pile too high
    Who's gonna see when I laugh
    Who's gonna come when I cry

Don't you worry baby now
It's gonna be all right
Just recall the words we said last night
And you will see it all as simple as a song
Keep your faith and your faith will keep you strong

# "Bad Mood"

School's out and I come on home to the ringing of the telephone
My mother is on the line, how you doing Mom? Oh I'm fine
Take out the trash, do your homework, feed the fish, and don't give your sister a hard
time
Gee, Mom, if you're wondering how I'm doing, oh I'm fine (not that you'd notice or
anything)

Bad mood, just another bad mood
Bad mood, just another bad mood
Bad mood, what's a kid to do
Bad mood, get in a bad mood, too?
How come lately everybody's always in a bad mood

Later that night the phone rings again, I pick it up hoping it's a friend
My Dad is on the phone, lately Dad's been living alone
He says son your mother says that lately your attitude has got to improve
I said Dad if you're so keen on what Mom says, how come you're not living here (oh
oh, trouble)

Bad mood, just another bad mood
Bad mood, just another bad mood
Bad mood, what's a kid to do
Bad mood, get in a bad mood, too?
How come lately everybody's always in a bad mood

Now my sis can be a pain in the neck, but she is human, so what the heck
It's a boring afternoon so I go walking up into her room
I say "sis, let's go down to the kitchen and I'll fix us some food"
She says, turn around walk out the door, close it and don't come back . . . I'm in a bad
mood
(Oh sorry I was born)

Bad mood, just another bad mood
Bad mood, just another bad mood
Bad mood, what's a kid to do
Bad mood, get in a bad mood, too?
How come lately everybody's always in a bad mood

# "So Am I"

So a hard thing happened to a pretty good kid
I tried to hold it inside and keep it all hid
I thought I was a loser I thought I was alone
But a lot of kids are having some trouble at home
We all got together and had a pretty good cry
We said life is tough . . .

So am I . . . so am I . . . so am I

I thought a lot of thoughts and cried a lot of tears
Heard my own hopes and . . . felt my own fears
I got what I needed in order to survive
I'm standing strong I'm alive I'm alive
You gotta do what you gotta do just to get by
Life is tough

So am I . . . so am I . . . so am I

Gotta hand, I'll take it
With your help I'm gonna make it
If you give me that tambourine
I'm gonna shake it while they play my song

I gotta little sister and she's got me
Together we try to be as tough as can be
We might fight sometimes but that's okay
We always make up the very next day
Just last week
She looked me in the eye she said life is tough

So am I . . . so am I . . . so am I.

Where's the hand. I'll take it.
Cause with your help I'm gonna make it
If you give me that tambourine
I'm gonna shake it all day long

I told you my story sang you my song
I hope it helps you feel better, helps you get along

Maybe some of these things have happened to you
You wondering how you're gonna get through
Just find yourself a mirror and look yourself in the eye and say life is tough …

So am I . . . so am I . . . so am I.

# "Everybody Needs A Friend"

I don't know why bad things happen to good people like you
But I do know there's a way to work things through
I'm not your boss and I don't want to tell you what to do
But everybody needs a friend

    You gotta find somebody to talk to
    You're gonna need somebody to talk to
    You gotta tell somebody what you've been through
    Everybody needs a friend

Now a friend is someone who is there to try and understand
A friend could be a boy or girl, a woman or a man
A friend is someone you can trust to lend a helping hand
And everybody needs a friend

    You gotta find somebody to talk to
    You're gonna need somebody to talk to
    You gotta tell somebody what you've been through
    Everybody needs a friend

Now some people feel funny 'bout when stuff goes on at home
And they're out there in the school yard feeling all alone
Times goes by and they just feel as lonely as a stone
Until the day they find a friend

    You gotta find somebody to talk to
    You're gonna need somebody to talk to
    You gotta tell somebody what you've been through
    Everybody needs a friend

Now you could be a football player you might be a movie star
You could ride around the world inside a big fat car
But someday something happens makes you wonder who you are
That's the day you need a friend

    You gotta find somebody to talk to
    You're gonna need somebody to talk to
    You gotta tell somebody what you've been through
    Everybody needs a friend

# "If You Believe In You"

After the storm the sun comes out
After the war there is peace
And if you've been trapped in your fear and doubt
You can be released
After you've lost your lonely way
And you just don't have a clue
You will find a brighter day
If you believe in you the way I do
If you believe in you the way I do

After the tears the smiles come back
And see you riding on a star
And if you fall off you will climb right back
That's just the way you are
And you will see the morning sun
Shining shining sweet and true
It's gonna feel like coming home
If you believe in you the way I do
If you believe in you the way I do

After you've been thrown like a stone and you've known the feeling
After you've been bounced like a ball so high in the sky so blue
After the time of hurting there is a time for healing
If you believe in you the way I do
If you believe in you the way I do

*Appendix*

# B

# SAMPLE FORMS

# Informational Sheet to Teachers and Staff for Possible Referrals to *Children of Divorce* Groups

Description of the *Children of Divorce* Group Program

Parental divorce is the issue of most concern for elementary school children (Nelson & Crawford, 1990). It is important to provide children of divorce with information about the following topics: separation, divorce, custody, visitation, parental fighting, parental dating, stepparents, and remarriage (Cebollero, Cruise, & Stollak, 1987; Rosenstein-Manner, 1990). Guldner and O'Connor (1991) stated that "where possible, group therapy for dealing with problems of children is the treatment of choice" (p. 184). Group counseling theory emphasizes the usefulness of a group setting in helping members to not feel isolated, to connect with and learn from others, to receive peer validation and support, and to normalize experiences (Gladding, 1991). Children of divorce, in particular, need a place to receive support, talk about their experiences of the divorce, realize that they are not alone in these experiences or feelings, and discuss ways to cope with the changes in their lives (Cantrell, 1986).

This children of divorce group will meet weekly for X weeks for 45 minutes. It will be a psychoeducational group that uses music to help children talk about their feelings and experiences related to divorce.

Procedures for Referring a Child to the *Children of Divorce* Group

Children who might benefit from this group include the following:

(1) Children who are 6 to 12 years old
(2) Children whose parents are divorced or separated
(3) Children who need to learn some ways to cope with their parents' divorce
(4) Children who would benefit from the support of other children in similar circumstances

To refer a child to this program, contact NAME OF COUNSELOR with the name of the child and reasons why this child would benefit from this group. The counselor will then inform the parent of the purpose of this group, and then the parent and the child will decide if they would like to participate.

NAME, ADDRESS, AND PHONE NUMBER OF COUNSELOR

# Information for Parents
# About *Children of Divorce* Groups

Purpose of the Group

Divorce has long-term implications for children as well as their parents. The National Center for Health estimates that one million divorces are granted each year in the United States. One million children experience the divorce of their parents each year. Parental divorce is the issue of most concern for elementary school children. Children of divorce need a place to receive support, talk about their experiences of the divorce, and realize that they are not alone in these experiences or feelings. This group will be a psychoeducational group that focuses on supporting children as they experience a divorce as well as promoting new skills to cope with the feelings and experiences related to the divorce.

We have formed this group for a couple of reasons. The first is that people, particularly children, are often uncomfortable talking about family stresses. This group will encourage them to talk about it and give them a safe place to do so. Second, children tend to talk to each other better than they do to adults, and so this will be a place for your child to express some of his or her thoughts and feelings about the divorce with other children who are having similar experiences. Hopefully, your child will find others that he or she can talk with long after the group ends. Because all children who are experiencing a divorce are encouraged to join, the groups are not designed just for those who are having problems.

What Is a Psychoeducational Group?

Psychoeducational groups emphasize the usefulness of a group setting to help children to not feel isolated, to connect with and learn from others, and to normalize some of their experiences. Psychoeducational groups, in contrast to counseling and therapy groups, focus specifically on the teaching of skills that may be helpful in difficult situations, such as communication skills, assertiveness, anger management, and expression of feelings.

The Group Counselors

The group counselors are responsible for using their knowledge of group dynamics to promote and facilitate individual and group growth. They are also responsible for creating an atmosphere of trust and support through specific ground rules, discussions of confidentiality, and their direction of each session. The group counselors are trained counselors who have a good understanding of the issues that children of divorce may be dealing with and a series of interventions that may be helpful to these children.

Topics to Be Addressed in This Group

It is important to provide children of divorce with information about the divorce process. The group leaders will provide some structure regarding the issues to be addressed in each session. Various topics may be covered in this group, including child self-esteem; acceptance of the family situation; feelings of guilt, shame, anger, and/or relief; custody; getting along with new siblings; parental fighting; parental dating; and remarriage.

This group will meet for X weeks starting XXX. For additional information, please contact XXX at XXX (school or agency) at this number:

# Information for Principals, Superintendents, and School Corporation Patrons About *Children of Divorce* Groups

Parental divorce is the issue of most concern for elementary school children (Nelson & Crawford, 1990). It is important to provide children of divorce with information about the following topics: separation, divorce, custody, visitation, parental fighting, parental dating, stepparents, and remarriage (Cebollero, Cruise, & Stollak, 1987; Rosenstein-Manner, 1990). Guldner and O'Connor (1991) stated that "where possible, group therapy for dealing with problems of children is the treatment of choice" (p. 184). Group counseling theory emphasizes the usefulness of a group setting in helping members to not feel isolated, to connect with and learn from others, to receive peer validation and support, and to normalize experiences (Gladding, 1991). Children of divorce, in particular, need a place to receive support, talk about their experiences of the divorce, realize that they are not alone in these experiences or feelings, and discuss ways to cope with the changes in their lives (Cantrell, 1986).

This children of divorce group will meet weekly for X weeks for 45 minutes. It will be a psychoeducational group that uses music to help children talk about their feelings and experiences related to divorce. The manual written by Dr. Janice DeLucia-Waack will be used as a framework for the group. Each session is outlined in detail. Material for the sessions is based on an extensive review of the literature related to group work and children of divorce and her counseling experience.

Psychoeducational groups emphasize the usefulness of a group setting to help children to not feel isolated, to connect with and learn from others, and to normalize some of their experiences. Psychoeducational groups, in contrast to counseling and therapy groups, focus specifically on the teaching of skills that may be helpful in difficult situations, such as communication skills, assertiveness, anger management, and expression of feelings.

The group counselors are responsible for using their knowledge of group dynamics to promote and facilitate individual and group growth. They are also responsible for creating an atmosphere of trust and support through specific ground rules, discussions of confidentiality, and their direction of each session. The group counselors are trained counselors who have a good understanding of the issues that children of divorce may be dealing with and a series of interventions that may be helpful to these children.

It is important to provide children of divorce with information about the divorce process. The group leaders will provide some structure regarding the issues to be addressed in each session. Various topics may be covered in this group, including child self-esteem; acceptance of the family situation; feelings of guilt, shame, anger, and/or relief; custody; getting along with new siblings; parental fighting; parental dating; and remarriage.

133

# Suggestions for Parents: Guidelines for Successful Postdivorce Parenting

These guidelines may help create a parenting partnership that is so critical for children of parents of divorce. The idea is to keep a relationship for the business of raising healthy children.

- *Your mutual concern is your children.* Decide to create a successful partnership for continuing to be parents despite the ending of the marriage.

- *Respect your children's relationship with your ex-spouse.* Your children did not divorce either parent. Encourage them to get over any feelings of estrangement from the other parent.

- Ask your ex-spouse to adopt these guidelines for working together as parents. If your ex-spouse refuses, *use these guidelines for yourself as much as possible.*

- *Be businesslike* with your former spouse. Test your own behavior by asking: Was I businesslike? Did I follow these guidelines?

- *Give your ex the benefit of the doubt* as to behavior, as you would a stranger. Do not assume anything based on past experience. There may be current reasons for your ex-spouse's behavior, thoughts, feelings, and decisions.

- *Do not expect approval from your ex-spouse.* Have your personal needs fulfilled elsewhere and with others.

- If you are able to *say something positive* about your ex-spouse's parenting, do so. Expressed appreciation, no matter how small, contributes to greater success of the parenting partnership.

- Do not discuss matters not related to the children unless your partner agrees to do so. *Respect your ex's privacy;* do not seek the details of his or her life or intrude on his or her territory.

- Test your ex-spouse's behavior **not** by how you feel but by the same standard: *Was his or her behavior businesslike?*

- *Make appointments to talk* about the children. Except for emergencies, call only during agreed on times. Ask if the time is convenient. If not, make an appointment for a time that is.

- *Be polite*. Do not use bad language or name call. Do not discuss issues while under the influence of alcohol or other drugs. If you feel yourself getting unbusinesslike, agree to talk at a later time.

- Before making decisions, *consult* with *your partner and the children* so the most workable decision can be made.

- Don't insist on what does not work. *Be flexible:* Commit yourself as much as you are able to and experiment to see what does work. Children's needs change as they get older.

- *You can only control your own thoughts, feelings, and behaviors.* Accept that you cannot control your ex-spouse's.

- *Make all arrangements clear* and follow up with written communication when possible (or make your own written agreement). Be clear and complete in your communication; include time, place, whether children will be fed or not, what clothes they need, etc. Communicate directly: **Do not** ask the children to do your business.

- *Keep arrangements.* Do not break appointments. Carry out what you promised. If you can't promise something, make it clear that you can't and say why.

- *Promote goodwill in the partnership.* Think of the importance of your investment and expected returns. The investment is what you will do for your children's happiness and success in life. The returns are comfort and security for your children, the children knowing their parents care enough to work together for them. A good working relationship with your former spouse will help make a better life for you and your children.

- Try not to compare households. Parents often have different parenting styles, financial resources, etc. Children can learn flexibility by experiencing different lifestyles.

From *The Boys and Girls Group: Divorce and Stepfamilies* (4th ed.), by Beech Acres Aring Institute, 1993, Cincinnati, OH: Beech Acres Aring Institute. Copyright 1993 by Beech Acres Aring Institute. Reprinted with permission.

# What Parents Can Do: Helpful Tips About Divorce

1. Tell the children about the divorce. Be honest and frank with them. Helping your children understand your divorce may be the most difficult task as parents.
2. Let the children know that both parents still love them even though they are living apart. Children of divorce often feel lost. They need assurance that they will be loved and cared for even after their parents separate.
3. Try to understand your own feelings about matters concerning the children. Although divorce ends a marriage, it should not put an end to the family.
4. Try to understand your own feelings and how to cope with them. Divorce has the potential for personal growth. It need not be emotionally destructive.
5. Help your children handle their feelings. Children react differently. The kind of help they need varies with their age.
6. Think about the good things you shared in your marriage. This can help you overcome the bitterness that often accompanies divorce.
7. If you are a visiting parent, be punctual and faithful in your appointments. Children are hurt by broken promises.
8. Tell the children only what they can grasp and understand. It is difficult for parents to know what to say and when.
9. Avoid saying unkind things to the children about the other parent. Children should be free to form their own opinions. They should be encouraged to see the good in each person.
10. Don't use the children to spy on the other parent's activities. Children should not be used as a "pipeline" for information
11. Keep the children out of your fighting. Children should not be caught in the battleground between their parents.
12. Try not to be a Santa Claus (if you are a visiting parent). This only makes it harder for the parent who has the day-to-day care.
13. Remember that you can't buy the children's affection through expensive gifts. The best gift is yourself, your time, and your love.
14. Don't involve the children with your new friends of the opposite sex. Children need time to adjust to the separation of their parents before they can be expected to accept third parties.
15. Seek professional help if your problems become more than you can handle.

# Parent Consent Form for
# *Children of Divorce* Groups

This is to certify that I, _____ , hereby voluntarily agree to allow my child, _____ , to participate in a children of divorce group under the leadership of _____ .

I understand that my child will attend a small group experience that focuses on various issues related to the divorce of his/her parents. Topics will include self-esteem; feelings of guilt, shame, and/or sadness; finding out about the divorce; visitation; and stepfamilies. The group will meet once a week for approximately X weeks for 45 minutes each week.

I understand that any information that I and my child provide will remain confidential except as discussed below.

I understand that if my child discloses that a minor is being abused or neglected in any way, the group facilitator and/or principal investigators are required by law to report this information to Child Protective Services and/or a law enforcement agency, even without my permission to do so.

I have been given the opportunity to ask any questions that I have. I am aware that if I have any more questions, I may contact XXX at XXX number.

_____

Parent's Signature                                                          Date

_____

Parent's Signature                                                          Date

# Consent Form for Children to Participate in *Children of Divorce* Groups

Counselor will read form to student to determine if the student would like to participate.

| Counselor Reads: | Child's Response: |
|---|---|
| Are your parents divorced? | Yes —— No —— |
| Does this make you sad sometimes? | Yes —— No —— |
| Do you think it might help to talk to some other children whose parents are also divorced? | Yes —— No —— |
| This group has children working together and a counselor to talk about how it feels to have parents who are divorced. You would meet every week for 45 minutes to talk about the divorce and try out some new strategies to cope. Would you like to be in a group like this? | Yes —— No —— |
| In order for us to learn about how to help children whose parents are divorced, we need to get some information from you about your family and your feelings and thoughts about the divorce and yourself. We would do this before the group starts. Would you be willing to give us this information? | Yes —— No —— |
| We would also like information about you from your parents. Is it OK for us to ask your parents for information about you? | Yes —— No —— |
| All of the information that you give us will be kept confidential. Do you know what confidential means? | Yes —— No —— |

*(If no, explain that confidential means that only the counselor with the group will know this information and that parents and teachers won't see the student's responses.)*

| Would you like to participate in this group where you can talk about your experiences with your parents' divorce? | Yes —— No —— |

If you would like to participate in this group, please sign your name below.

_____

# Sample List of Questions
# to Ask in Interview

Hello, my name is XXX, and I am the counselor here. I am starting a group for children who have experienced a divorce or separation in their families and would like a safe place to talk about it. Hopefully, 5 or 6 children will want to talk about it, and we will do some really neat stuff when we get together. I have some songs that kids sing about divorce and some fun activities to do that will help to talk about and problem solve about the divorce. Would you be interested in joining? It would be kind of like a club; we would decide on a name and rules and then do some fun stuff together.

I do need to know some stuff about you and your parents' situation to plan for this group and choose activities. Can you tell me about your family situation now?

How has it changed in the last few years?

Try to get information about the following topics:

> When did the parents divorce or separate? Dates of both, if applicable?
> With whom do they live?
> What is the custody arrangement?
> How do the parents interact with each other?
> Stepparents? Are parents dating/living with someone else?
>
> Names, ages, and gender of brothers and sisters?
> Names, ages, and gender of new siblings?
> Who lives with whom?
> How do they get along with siblings?
> Whom can they talk to about the divorce?
>
> Support system of other family members and/or friends whom they can talk to about the divorce?
>
> Happy memories before the divorce?
> Sad memories before the divorce?
> Happy and sad memories since the divorce?
>
> What topics do they want to talk about in the group?

# C

# SAMPLE ASSESSMENTS

# Initial Assessment Instrument*

|  | YES | NO |
|---|---|---|
| 1. My parents live in different houses. | ____ | ____ |
| 2. My parents are divorced. | ____ | ____ |
| 3. I live with my mom. | ____ | ____ |
| 4. I live with my dad. | ____ | ____ |
| 5. My mom is remarried. | ____ | ____ |
| 6. My dad is remarried. | ____ | ____ |

**Put a check in the space if the sentence describes something that is HARD for you.**

____  7. There have been a lot of problems in our family since Mom and Dad don't get along.      *Divorce Experience*

____  8. Sometimes these problems seem like my fault.

____  9. There has been a lot of fighting between Mom and Dad.      *Parents' Fighting*

____ 10. I worry that someone will get hurt when Mom and Dad fight.

____ 11. I worry about what's going on with the lawyers or in court.      *Legal Aspects*

____ 12. I think things about the judge and the courts are confusing.

____ 13. Mom or Dad asks me to tell my other parent things I don't want to say.      *Caught in the Middle*

____ 14. Mom or Dad says bad things about my other parent.

*Labels in italics in the right-hand column for Questions 7 to 26 indicate important issues to be addressed in sessions.

_____ 15. I don't see one parent very much.

_____ 16. I miss one of my parents.

*Maintaining Parent Relationships*

_____ 17. We have money problems since Mom and Dad don't get along.

_____ 18. There have been a lot of changes in my life because Mom and Dad don't get along.

*Changes*

_____ 19. Mom or Dad dates new people.

_____ 20. Mom or Dad lives with his/her girlfriend or boyfriend.

*Parents' New Partners*

_____ 21. I live in a stepfamily.

_____ 22. I have stepbrothers or stepsisters.

*Stepfamilies*

_____ 23. I have a lot of different feelings about the divorce.

_____ 24. Sometimes I am not sure what I feel.

*Feelings*

_____ 25. Sometimes I am not sure how to talk about my feelings.

_____ 26. I have things that I want to say to Mom or Dad that I don't know how.

*Communication*

Name _____ Date _____

# Assessment of Critical Incidents in Group

# WHAT WAS HELPFUL TODAY?

Of all the things that happened today in our group, what was the most helpful? Briefly describe what happened.


Why was it so helpful?


---

This can be analyzed in terms of Yalom's (1995) therapeutic factors.

1. Altruism

2. Catharsis

3. Cohesiveness

4. Development of Socializing Techniques

5. Existential Factors

6. Imparting of Information

7. Initiative Behavior

8. Instillation of Hope

9. Interpersonal Learning

10. The Corrective Recapitulation of the Primary Family Group

11. Self-Understanding

12. Universality

# Assessment of Weekly Song Usage

Name: _____ Week: _____

How many times this week did you listen to each of the following songs?

_____ And I Need A Lot Of Love

_____ I Tried

_____ Perfect People

_____ I Am A Kid

_____ Bad Mood

_____ Everybody Needs A Friend

_____ If You Believe In You

_____ Divorce

_____ Is It My Fault?

_____ Casey The Clown

_____ I Worry

_____ So Am I

What else did you do this week related to this group or to the divorce?

# Children's Beliefs About Parental Divorce Scale

By Berthold Berg, PhD and Lawrence Kurdek, PhD

NAME _____ SEX: BOY GIRL

AGE _____ DATE OF BIRTH __ __ __ GRADE _____

## INSTRUCTIONS

On the following pages are some statements about children and their separated parents. Some of them are TRUE about how you think or feel, so you will want to check YES. Some are NOT TRUE about how you think or feel, so you will want to check NO. There are no right or wrong answers. Your answers will just tell us some of the things you are thinking now about your parents' separation.

PRA _____ PB _____ FA _____ HR _____ MB _____ SB _____ TOT _____

YES NO  1. It would upset me if other kids asked a lot of questions about my parents.

YES NO  2. It was usually my father's fault when my parents had a fight.

YES NO  3. I sometimes worry that both my parents will want to live without me.

YES NO  4. When my family was unhappy, it was because of my mother.

YES NO  5. My parents will always live apart.

YES NO  6. My parents often argue with each other after I misbehave.

YES NO  7. I like talking to my friends as much now as I used to.

YES NO  8. My father is usually a nice person.

YES NO  9. It's possible that both my parents will never want to see me again.

YES NO  10. My mother is usually a nice person.

YES NO  11. If I behave better, I might be able to bring my family back together.

YES NO  12. My parents would probably be happier if I were never born.

YES NO  13. I like playing with my friends as much now as I used to.

YES NO  14. When my family was unhappy, it was usually because of something my father said or did.

YES   NO   15. I sometimes worry that I'll be left all alone.

YES   NO   16. Often I have a bad time when I'm with my mother.

YES   NO   17. My family will probably do things together just like before.

YES   NO   18. My parents probably argue more when I'm with them than when I'm gone.

YES   NO   19. I'd rather be alone than play with other kids.

YES   NO   20. My father caused most of the trouble in my family.

YES   NO   21. I feel that my parents still love me.

YES   NO   22. My mother caused most of the trouble in my family.

YES   NO   23. My parents will probably see that they have made a mistake and get back together.

YES   NO   24. My parents are happier when I'm with them than when I'm not.

YES   NO   25. My friends and I do many things together.

YES   NO   26. There are a lot of things about my father I like.

YES   NO   27. I sometimes think that one day I may have to go live with a friend or relative.

YES   NO   28. My mother is more good than bad.

YES   NO   29. I sometimes think that my parents will one day live together again.

YES   NO   30. I can make my parents unhappy with each other by what I say or do.

YES   NO   31. My friends understand how I feel about my parents.

YES   NO   32. My father is more good than bad.

YES   NO   33. I feel my parents still like me.

YES   NO   34. There are a lot of things about my mother I like.

YES   NO   35. I sometimes think that once my parents realize how much I want them to, they'll live together again.

YES   NO   36. My parents would probably still be living together if it weren't for me.

# Background Information Sheet

(To be completed by the parent)

Age: _____ Sex: _____ Race: _____

Whom does the child live with? _____

Name, age, and sex of brothers and sisters who live with child:

_____

_____

_____

_____

_____

Name, age, and sex of brothers and sisters who don't live with child:

_____

_____

_____

_____

_____

Issues/concerns related to divorce/separation for the child:

_____

_____

_____

_____

_____

_____

**About Mother:**

Age: _____ Sex: _____ Race: _____

Occupation:

Current marital status:

**About Father:**

Age: _____    Sex: _____    Race: _____

Occupation:

Current marital status:

**About the Divorce/Separation:**

Date of separation: _____    Date of divorce: _____

Visitation guidelines set by court: _____

Actual visitation schedule in the last year: _____

Anything else that you think the group leaders should know to help your child in this group: _____

_____

_____

_____

# Evaluation of
## *Children of Divorce* Group Session

(By the Group Leader)

Session #

Session Used Manual:

Children Present:

How did the children respond to the session?

Were they able to follow the directions?

What did they talk about related to the divorce?

Their feelings?

How did they cope with the divorce?

What did they learn from each other?

I thought that this went well because ...

I thought this activity could have been improved by ...

I would change ...

Additional comments:

Issues/topics to address at next session:

# Evaluation at the End of Group by Members

(For Grades K–2)

Name: _____  Date: _____

Group Leader: _____

| I think the group can help kids: | Yes | Don't know | No |
|---|---|---|---|
| 1. Feel better about themselves | ____ | ____ | ____ |
| 2. Get their feelings out | | | |
| 3. Better understand changes in their families | ____ | ____ | ____ |
| 4. Learn new things that will help them deal with the problems in their family | ____ | ____ | ____ |
| 5. Overall the group was helpful | ____ | ____ | ____ |
| 6. The group leader did a good job | ____ | ____ | ____ |

7. Something I learned in group is _____

_____

_____

_____

_____

8. If I had a friend who had family changes like mine, I would tell him/her to join a group.

Yes _____  No _____  Maybe _____

9. Ideas I have for making the group better are _____

_____

_____

# Evaluation at the End of Group by Members

## (Grades 3 and Up)

Name: _____  Date: _____

Group Leader: _____

| I think the group can help kids: | Yes | Most Yes | Don't Know | Most No | No |
|---|---|---|---|---|---|
| 1. Feel better about themselves | 5 | 4 | 3 | 2 | 1 |
| 2. Get their feelings out | 5 | 4 | 3 | 2 | 1 |
| 3. Better understand changes in their families | 5 | 4 | 3 | 2 | 1 |
| 4. Learn new things that will help them deal with the problems in their family | 5 | 4 | 3 | 2 | 1 |
| 5. Overall the group was helpful | 5 | 4 | 3 | 2 | 1 |
| 6. The group leader did a good job | 5 | 4 | 3 | 2 | 1 |

7. Something I learned in group is _____

_____

_____

_____

8. If I had a friend who had family changes like mine, I would tell him/her to join a group.

Yes _____    No _____    Maybe _____

9. Ideas I have for making the group better are _____

_____

_____

From *The Boys and Girls Group: Divorce and Stepfamilies* (4th ed.), by Beech Acres Aring Institute, 1993, Cincinnati, OH: Beech Acres Aring Institute. Copyright 1993 by Beech Acres Aring Institute. Reprinted with permission.

# Parent's Evaluation at the End of Group

Parents: Please complete this form without talking to your child to reflect what you think has been valuable for your child.

| 1. Parts of the group my child seems to like were: | A Lot | A Little | Not at All |
|---|---|---|---|
| Listening to other children talk about their lives | —— | —— | —— |
| Having others to talk to about his/her own experiences | —— | —— | —— |
| The role-plays (or puppet plays) about the divorce situation | —— | —— | —— |
| Worksheets | —— | —— | —— |
| Learning more about how families change | —— | —— | —— |
| Being with other children who experienced a similar situation | —— | —— | —— |
| The group leaders | —— | —— | —— |
| Anything else? | —— | —— | —— |

| 2. I think the group can help children: | A Lot | A Little | Not at All |
|---|---|---|---|
| Feel better about themselves | —— | —— | —— |
| Understand their parents better | —— | —— | —— |
| Communicate or get along better with their mother | —— | —— | —— |

# D

# ASGW PROFESSIONAL STANDARDS FOR THE TRAINING OF GROUP WORKERS

# PROFESSIONAL STANDARDS FOR
# THE TRAINING OF GROUP WORKERS

Revision Approved by the Executive Board, January 22, 2000
Prepared by F. Robert Wilson and Lynn S. Rapin, Co-Chairs,
and Lynn Haley-Banez, Member, ASGW Standards Committee
Consultants: Robert K. Conyne and Donald E. Ward

### Preamble

For nearly two decades, the Association for Specialists in Group Work (herein referred to as ASGW or as the Association) has promulgated professional standards for the training of group workers. In the early 1980s, the Association published the ASGW Training Standards for Group Counselors (1983) which established nine knowledge competencies, seventeen competencies, and clock-hour baselines for various aspects of supervised clinical experience in group counseling. The focus on group counseling embodied in these standards mirrored the general conception of the time that whatever counselors did with groups of individuals should properly be referred to as group counseling.

New ground was broken in the 1990 revision of the ASGW Professional Standards for the Training of Group Workers with (a) the articulation of the term, *group work*, to capture the variety of ways in which counselors work with groups, (b) differentiation of core training, deemed essential for all counselors, from specialization training required of those intending to engage in group work as part of their professional practice, and (c) the differentiation among four distinct group work specializations: task and work group facilitation, group psychoeducational, group counseling, and group psychotherapy. Over the ten years in which these standards have been in force, commentary and criticism has been elicited through discussion groups at various regional and national conferences and through published analyses in the Association's journal, the *Journal for Specialists in Group Work*.

In this Year-2000 revision of the ASGW Professional Standards for the Training of Group Workers, the foundation established by the 1990 training standards has been preserved and refined by application of feedback received through public discussion and scholarly debate. The Year-2000 revision maintains and strengthens the distinction between core and specialization training with requirements for core training and aspirational guidelines for specialization training. Further, the definitions of group work specializations have been expanded and clarified. Evenness of application of training standards across the specialization has been assured by creating a single set of guidelines for all four specializations with specialization specific detail being supplied where necessary. Consistent with both the pattern for training standards established by the Council for Accreditation of Counseling and Related Educational Program accreditation standards and past editions of the ASGW training standards, the Year-

2000 revision addresses both content and clinical instruction. Content instruction is described in terms of both course work requirements and knowledge objectives while clinical instruction is articulated in experiential requirements and skill objectives. This revision of the training standards was informed by and profits from the seminal ASGW Best Practice Guidelines (1998) and the ASGW Principles for Diversity-Competent Group Workers (1999).

Although each of these documents have their own form of organization, all address the group work elements of planning, performing, and processing and the ethical and diversity-competent treatment of participants in group activities.

## Purpose

The purpose of the Professional Standards for the Training of Group Workers is to provide guidance to counselor training programs in the construction of their curricula for graduate programs in counseling (e.g., master's, specialist, and doctoral degrees and other forms of advanced graduate study). Specifically, core standards express the Association's view on the minimum training in group work all programs in counseling should provide for all graduates of their entry level, master's degree programs in counseling, and specialization standards provide a framework for documenting the training philosophy, objectives, curriculum, and outcomes for each declared specialization program.

**Core Training in Group Work.** All counselors should possess a set of core competencies in general group work. The Association for Specialists in Group Work advocates for the incorporation of core group work competencies as part of required entry level training in all counselor preparation programs. The Association's standards for core training are consistent with and provide further elaboration of the standards for accreditation of entry level counseling programs identified by the Council for Accreditation of Counseling and Related Educational Programs (CACREP, 1994). Mastery of the core competencies detailed in the ASGW training standards will prepare the counselor to understand group process phenomena and to function more effectively in groups in which the counselor is a member. Mastery of basic knowledge and skill in group work provides a foundation which specialty training can extend but does not qualify one to independently practice any group work specialty.

**Specialist Training in Group Work.** The independent practice of group work requires training beyond core competencies. ASGW advocates that independent practitioners of group work must possess advanced competencies relevant to the particular kind of group work practice in which the group work student wants to specialize (e.g., facilitation of task groups, group psychoeducational, group counseling, or group psychotherapy). To encourage program creativity in development of specialization training, the specialization guidelines do not prescribe minimum trainee competencies. Rather, the guidelines establish a framework within which programs can develop unique training experiences utilizing scientific foundations and best practices to achieve their training objectives. In providing these guidelines for specialized training, ASGW makes no presumption that a graduate program in counseling must provide training in a group work specialization nor that adequate training in a specialization can be accomplished solely within a well-rounded master's degree program in counseling. To provide adequate specialization training, completion of post-master's options such as certificates of post-master's study or doctoral degrees may be required. Further, there is no presumption that an individual who may have received adequate training in a given declared specialization will be prepared to function effectively with all group situations in which the graduate may want to or be required to work. It is recognized that the characteristics of specific client populations and employment settings vary widely. Additional training beyond that which was acquired in a specific graduate program may be necessary for optimal, diversity-competent, group work practice with a given population in a given setting.

## Definitions

**Group Work:** is a broad professional practice involving the application of knowledge and skill in group facilitation to assist an interdependent collection of people to reach their mutual goals which may be interpersonal, intrapersonal, or work-related. The goals of the group may include the accomplishment of tasks related to work, education, personal development, personal and interpersonal problem solving, or remediation of mental and emotional disorders.

**Core Training in Group Work:** includes knowledge, skills, and experiences deemed necessary for general competency for all master's degree prepared counselors. ASGW advocates for all counselor preparation programs to provide core training in group work regardless of whether the program intends to prepare trainees for independent practice in a group work specialization. Core training in group work is considered a necessary prerequisite for advanced practice in group work.

**Specialization Training in Group Work:** includes knowledge, skills, and experiences deemed necessary for counselors to engage in independent practice of group work. Four areas of advanced practice, referred to as specializations, are identified: Task Group Facilitation, Group Psychoeducational, Group Counseling, and Group Psychotherapy. This list is not presumed to be exhaustive and while there may be no sharp boundaries between the specializations, each has recognizable characteristics that have professional utility. The definitions for these group work specializations have been built upon the American Counseling Association's model definition of counseling (adopted by the ACA Governing Council in 1997), describing the methods typical of the working stage of the group being defined and the typical purposes to which those methods are put and the typical populations served by those methods. Specialized training presumes mastery of prerequisite core knowledge, skills, and experiences.

### Specialization in Task and Work Group Facilitation:
- The application of principles of normal human development and functioning
- through group based educational, developmental, and systemic strategies
- applied in the context of here-and-now interaction
- that promote efficient and effective accomplishment of group tasks
- among people who are gathered to accomplish group task goals.

## Specialization in Psychoeducational Group Leadership:

- The application of principles of normal human development and functioning
- through group based educational and developmental strategies applied in the context of here-and-now interaction that promote personal and interpersonal growth and development and the prevention of future difficulties among people who may be at risk for the development of personal or interpersonal problems or who seek enhancement of personal qualities and abilities.

## Specialization in Group Counseling:

- The application of principles of normal human development and functioning through group based cognitive, affective, behavioral, or systemic intervention strategies applied in the context of here-and-now interaction that address personal and interpersonal problems of living and promote personal and interpersonal growth and development among people who may be experiencing transitory maladjustment, who are at risk for the development of personal or interpersonal problems, or who seek enhancement of personal qualities and abilities.

## Specialization in Group Psychotherapy:

- The application of principles of normal and abnormal human development and functioning
- through group based cognitive, affective, behavioral, or systemic intervention strategies
- applied in the context of negative emotional arousal
- that address personal and interpersonal problems of living, remediate perceptual and cognitive distortions or repetitive patterns of dysfunctional behavior, and promote personal and interpersonal growth and development
- among people who may be experiencing severe and/or chronic maladjustment.

### Core Training Standards

I. **Coursework and Experiential Requirements**

   A. *Coursework Requirements.* Core training shall include at least one graduate course in group work that addresses such as but not limited to scope of practice, types of group work, group development, group process and dynamics, group leadership, and standards of training and practice for group workers.

   B. *Experiential Requirements.* Core training shall include a minimum of 10 clock hours (20 clock hours recommended) observation of and participation in a group experience as a group member and/or as a group leader.

II. **Knowledge and Skill Objectives**

   A. **Nature and Scope of Practice**

      1. *Knowledge Objectives.* Identify and describe:

         a. the nature of group work and the various specializations within group work

    b. theories of group work including commonalties and distinguishing characteristics among the various specializations within group work

    c. research literature pertinent to group work and its specializations

  2. *Skill Objectives.* Demonstrate skill in:

    a. preparing a professional disclosure statement for practice in a chosen area of specialization

    b. applying theoretical concepts and scientific findings to the design of a group and the interpretation of personal experiences in a group

B. **Assessment of Group Members and the Social Systems in Which They Live and Work**

  1. *Knowledge Objectives.* Identify and describe:

    a. principles of assessment of group functioning in group work

    b. use of personal contextual factors (e.g., family-of-origin, neighborhood-of-residence, organizational membership, cultural membership) in interpreting behavior of members in a group

  2. *Skill Objectives.* Demonstrate skill in:

    a. observing and identifying group process

    b. observing the personal characteristics of individual members in a group

    c. developing hypotheses about the behavior of group members

    d. employing contextual factors (e.g., family-of-origin, neighborhood-of-residence, organizational membership, cultural membership) in interpretation of individual and group data

C. **Planning Group Interventions**

  1. *Knowledge Objectives.* Identify and describe:

    a. environmental contexts, which affect planning for group interventions

    b. the impact of group member diversity (e.g., gender, culture, learning style, group climate preference) on group member behavior and group process and dynamics in group work

    c. principles of planning for group work

  2. *Skill Objectives.* Demonstrate skill in:

    a. collaborative consultation with targeted populations to enhance ecological validity of planned group interventions

    b. planning for a group work activity including such aspects as developing overarching purpose, establishing goals and objectives, detailing methods to be used in achieving goals and objectives, determining methods for outcome assessment, and verifying ecological validity of plan

D. **Implementation of Group Interventions**

  1. *Knowledge Objectives.* Identify and describe:

    a. principles of group formation including recruiting, screening, and selecting group members

    b. principles for effective performance of group leadership functions

    c. therapeutic factors within group work and when group work approaches are indicated and contraindicated

      d. principles of group dynamics including group process components, developmental stage theories, group member roles, group member behaviors

  2. **Skill Objectives.** Demonstrate skill in:

      a. encouraging participation of group members

      b. attending to, describing, acknowledging, confronting, understanding, and responding empathetically to group member behavior

      c. attending to, acknowledging, clarifying, summarizing, confronting, and responding empathetically to group member statements

      d. attending to, acknowledging, clarifying, summarizing, confronting, and responding empathetically to group themes

      e. eliciting information from and imparting information to group members

      f. no providing appropriate self-disclosure

      g. maintaining group focus; keeping a group on task

      h. giving and receiving feedback in a group setting

**E. Leadership and Co-Leadership**

  1. **Knowledge Objectives.** Identify and describe:

      a. group leadership styles and approaches

      b. group work methods including group worker orientations and specialized group leadership behaviors

      c. principles of collaborative group processing

  2. **Skill Objectives.** To the extent opportunities for leadership or co-leadership are provided, demonstrate skill in:

      a. engaging in reflective evaluation of one's personal leadership style and approach

      b. working cooperatively with a co-leader and/or group members

      c. engaging in collaborative group processing.

**F. Evaluation**

  1. **Knowledge Objectives.** Identify and describe:

      a. methods for evaluating group process in group work

      b. methods for evaluating outcomes in group work

  2. **Skill Objectives.** Demonstrate skill in:

      a. contributing to evaluation activities during group participation

      b. engaging in self-evaluation of personally selected performance goals

**G. Ethical Practice, Best Practice, Diversity-Competent Practice**

  1. **Knowledge Objectives.** Identify and describe:

      a. ethical considerations unique to group work

      b. best practices in group work

      c. diversity-competent group work

  2. **Skill Objectives.** Demonstrate skill in:

      a. evidencing ethical practice in planning, observing, and participating in group activities

      b. evidencing best practice in planning, observing, and participating in group activities

c. evidencing diversity-competent practice in planning, observing, and participating in group activities

## Specialization Guidelines

### I. Overarching Program Characteristics

A. The program has a clearly specified philosophy of training for the preparation of specialists for independent practice of group work in one of the forms of group work recognized by the Association (i.e., task and work group facilitation, group psychoeducational, group counseling, or group psychotherapy).

  1. The program states an explicit intent to train group workers in one or more of the group work specializations.

  2. The program states an explicit philosophy of training, based on the science of group work, by which it intends to prepare students for independent practice in the declared specialization.

B. For each declared specialization, the program specifies education and training objectives in terms of the competencies expected of students completing the specialization training. These competencies are consistent with

  1. the program's philosophy and training model,

  2. the substantive area(s) relevant for best practice of the declared specialization area, and standards for competent, ethical, and diversity sensitive practice of group work

C. For each declared specialization, the program specifies a sequential, cumulative curriculum, expanding in breadth and depth, and designed to prepare students for independent practice of the specialization and relevant credentialing.

D. For each declared specialization, the program documents achievement of training objectives in terms of student competencies.

### II. Recommended Coursework and Experience

A. *Coursework.* Specialization training may include coursework which provides the student with a broad foundation in the group work domain in which the student seeks specialized training:

  1. *Task/Work Group Facilitation:* coursework includes but is not limited to organizational development, management and consultation, theory and practice of task/work group facilitation

  2. *Group Psychoeducational:* coursework includes but is not limited to organizational development, school and community counseling/psychology, health promotion, marketing, program development and evaluation, organizational consultation, theory and practice of group psychoeducational

  3. *Group Counseling:* coursework includes but is not limited to normal human development, health promotion, theory and practice of group counseling

  4. *Group Psychotherapy:* coursework includes but is not be limited to normal and abnormal human development, assessment and diagnosis of mental and emotional disorders, treatment of psychopathology, theory and practice of group psychotherapy

**B. *Experience.*** Specialization training includes

1. *Task/Work Group Facilitation:* a minimum of 30 clock hours (45 clock hours recommended) supervised practice facilitating or conducting an intervention with a task or work group appropriate to the age and clientele of the group leader's specialty area (e.g., school counseling, student development counseling, community counseling, mental health counseling)

2. *Group Psychoeducational:* a minimum of 30 clock hours (45 clock hours recommended) supervised practice conducting a psychoeducational group appropriate to the age and clientele of the group leader's specialty area (e.g., school counseling, student development counseling, community counseling, mental health counseling)

3. *Group Counseling:* a minimum of 45 clock hours (60 clock hours recommended) supervised practice conducting a counseling group appropriate to the age and clientele of the group leader's specialty area (e.g., school counseling, student development counseling, community counseling, mental health counseling)

4. *Group Psychotherapy:* a minimum of 45 clock hours (60 clock hours recommended) supervised practice conducting a psychotherapy group appropriate to the age and clientele of the group leader's specialty area (e.g., mental health counseling)

## III. Knowledge and Skill Elements

In achieving its objectives, the program has and implements a clear and coherent curriculum plan that provides the means whereby all students can acquire and demonstrate substantial understanding of and competence in the following areas:

**A. Nature and Scope of Practice**

The program states a clear expectation that its students will limit their independent practice of group work to those specialization areas for which they have been appropriately trained and supervised.

**B. Assessment of Group Members and the Social Systems in Which They Live and Work**

All graduates of specialization training will understand and demonstrate competence in the use of assessment instruments and methodologies for assessing individual group member characteristics development, group dynamics, and process phenomena relevant for the program's declared specialization area(s). Studies should include but are not limited to:

1. methods of screening and assessment of populations, groups, and individual members who are or may be targeted for intervention

2. methods for observation of group member behavior during group interventions

3. methods of assessment of group development, process, and outcomes

**C. Planning Group Interventions**

All graduates of specialization training will understand and demonstrate competence in planning group interventions consistent with the program's declared specialization areas(s). Studies should include but are not limited to:

1. establishing the overarching purpose for the intervention
2. identifying goals and objectives for the intervention
3. detailing methods to be employed in achieving goals and objectives during the intervention
4. selecting methods for examining group process during group meetings, between group sessions, and at the completion of the group intervention
5. preparing methods for helping members derive meaning from their within-group experiences and transfer within-group learning to real-world circumstances
6. determining methods for measuring outcomes during and following the intervention
7. verifying ecological validity of plans for the intervention

D. **Implementation of Group Interventions**

All graduates of specialization training will understand and demonstrate competence implementing group interventions consistent with the program's declared specialization area(s). Studies should include but are not limited to:

1. principles of group formation including recruiting, screening, selection, and orientation of group members
2. standard methods and procedures for group facilitation
3. selection and use of referral sources appropriate to the declared specialization
4. identifying and responding constructively to extra-group factors which may influence the success of interventions
5. applying the major strategies, techniques, and procedures
6. adjusting group pacing relative to the stage of group development
7. identifying and responding constructively to critical incidents
8. identifying and responding constructively to disruptive members
9. helping group members attribute meaning to and integrate and apply learning
10. responding constructively to psychological emergencies
11. involving group members in within group session processing and ongoing planning

E. **Leadership and Co-Leadership**

All graduates of specialization training will understand and demonstrate competence in pursuing personal competence as a leader and in selecting and managing the interpersonal relationship with a co-leader for group interventions consistent with the program's declared specialization area(s). Studies should include but are not limited to:

1. characteristics and skills of effective leaders
2. relationship skills required of effective co-leaders
3. processing skills required of effective co-leaders

## F. Evaluation

All graduates of specialization training will understand and demonstrate competence in evaluating group interventions consistent with the program's declared specialization area(s). Studies should include but are not limited to methods for evaluating participant outcomes and participant satisfaction.

## G. Ethical Practice, Best Practice, Diversity-Competent Practice

All graduates of specialization training will understand and demonstrate consistent effort to comply with principles of ethical, best practice, and diversity-competent practice of group work consistent with the program's declared specialization area(s). Studies should include but are not limited to:

1. ethical considerations unique to the program's declared specialization area
2. best practices for group work within the program's declared specialization area
3. diversity issues unique to the program's declared specialization area

## Implementation Guidelines

Implementation of the Professional Standards for the Training of Group Workers requires a commitment by a program's faculty and a dedication of program resources to achieve excellence in preparing all counselors at core competency level and in preparing counselors for independent practice of group work. To facilitate implementation of the training standards, the Association offers the following guidelines.

### Core Training in Group Work

Core training in group work can be provided through a single, basic course in group theory and process. This course should include the elements of content instruction detailed below and may also include the required clinical instruction component.

### Content Instruction

Consistent with accreditation standards (CACREP, 1994, Standard II.J.4) study in the area of groups, work should provide an understanding of the types of group work (e.g., facilitation of task groups, psychoeducational groups, counseling groups, psychotherapy groups); group development, group dynamics, and group leadership styles; and group leadership methods and skills. More explicitly, studies should include, but not be limited to the following:

- principles of group dynamics including group process components, developmental stage theories, and group member's roles and behaviors;
- group leadership styles and approaches including characteristics of various types of group leaders and leadership styles;
- theories of group counseling including commonalties, distinguishing characteristics, and pertinent research and literature;
- group work methods including group leader orientations and behaviors, ethical standards, appropriate selection criteria and methods, and methods of evaluating effectiveness;
- approaches used for other types of group work, including task groups, prevention groups, support groups, and therapy groups; and

- skills in observing member behavior and group process, empathic responding, confronting, self-disclosing, focusing, protecting, recruiting and selecting members, opening and closing sessions, managing, explicit and implicit teaching, modeling, giving and receiving feedback

### Clinical Instruction

Core group training requires a minimum of 10 clock hours of supervised practice (20 clock hours of supervised practice is recommended). Consistent with CACREP standards for accreditation, the supervised experience provides the student with direct experiences as a participant in a small group, and may be met either in the basic course in group theory and practice or in a specially conducted small group designed for the purpose of meeting this standard. (CACREP, 1994, Standard II.D). In arranging for and conducting this group experience, care must be taken by program faculty to assure that the ACA ethical standard for dual relationships and ASGW standards for best practice are observed.

### Specialist Training in Group Work

Though ASGW advocates that all counselor training programs provide all counseling students with core group work training, specialization training is elective. If a counselor training program chooses to offer specialization training (e.g., task group facilitation, group psychoeducational, group counseling, group psychotherapy), ASGW urges institutions to develop their curricula consistent with the ASGW standards for that specialization.

### Content Instruction

Each area of specialization has its literature. In addition to basic course work in group theory and process, each specialization requires additional coursework providing specialized knowledge necessary for professional application of the specialization:

- **Task Group Facilitation:** coursework in such areas as organization development, consultation, management, or sociology so students gain a basic understanding of organizations and how task groups function within them.
- **Group Psychoeducational:** coursework in community psychology, consultation, health promotion, marketing, curriculum design to prepare students to conduct structured consciousness raising and skill training groups in such areas as stress management, wellness, anger control and assertiveness training, problem solving.
- **Group Counseling:** coursework in normal human development, family development and family counseling, assessment and problem identification of problems in living, individual counseling, and group counseling, including training experiences in personal growth or counseling group.
- **Group Psychotherapy:** coursework in abnormal human development, family pathology and family therapy, assessment and diagnosis of mental and emotional disorders, individual therapy, and group therapy, including training experiences in a therapy group.

### Clinical Instruction:

For Task Group Facilitation and Group Psychoeducational, group specialization training recommends a minimum of 30 clock hours of supervised practice (45 clock

hours of supervised practice is strongly suggested). Because of the additional difficulties presented by Group Counseling and Group Psychotherapy, a minimum of 45
clock hours of supervised practice is recommended (60 clock hours of supervised practice is strongly suggested). Consistent with CACREP standards for accreditation,
supervised experience should provide an opportunity for the student to perform under
supervision a variety of activities that a professional counselor would perform in conducting group work consistent with a given specialization (i.e., assessment of group
members and the social systems in which they live and work, planning group interventions, implementing group interventions, leadership and co-leadership, and
within-group, between-group, and end-of-group processing and evaluation).

In addition to courses offering content and experience related to a given specialization, supervised clinical experience should be obtained in practical and internship
experience. Following the model provided by CACREP for master's practical, we recommend that one quarter of all required supervised clinical experience be devoted to
group work:

- **Master's Practicum:** At least 10 clock hours of the required 40 clock hours of
  direct service should be spent in supervised leadership or co-leadership experience
  in group work, typically in Task Group Facilitation, Group Psychoeducational, or
  Group Counseling (at the master's practicum level, experience in Group Psychotherapy would be unusual) (CACREP, 1994, Standard III.H.1).
- **Master's Internship:** At least 60 clock hours of the required 240 clock hours of direct
  services should be spent in supervised leadership or co-leadership in group work consistent with the program's specialization offering(s) (i.e., in Task Group Facilitation,
  Group Psychoeducational, Group Counseling, or Group Psychotherapy).
- **Doctoral Internship:** At least 150 clock hours of the required 600 clock hours of
  direct service should be spent in supervised leadership or co-leadership in group work
  consistent with the program's specialization offering(s) (i.e., in Task Group Facilitation, Group Psychoeducational, Group Counseling, or Group Psychotherapy).

### References

Association for Specialists in Group Work. (1983). *ASGW Professional Standards for Group
Counseling.* Alexandria, VA: Author.

Association for Specialists in Group Work. (1990). *Professional Standards for the Training of
Group Workers.* Alexandria, VA: Author.

Association for Specialists in Group Work. (1998). ASGW Best Practice Guidelines. *Journal for
Specialists in Group Work, 23,* 237–244.

Association for Specialists in Group Work. (1999). ASGW Principles for Diversity-Competent
Group Workers. *Journal for Specialists in Group Work, 24,* 7–14.

Council for Accreditation of Counseling and Related Educational Programs (CACREP).
(1994). *CACREP accreditation standards and procedures manual.* Alexandria, VA: Author.

# E

# ASGW Best Practice Guidelines

# BEST PRACTICE GUIDELINES

Approved by the ASGW Executive Board, March 29, 1998
Prepared by Lynn S. Rapin and Linda Keel, ASGW Ethics Committee Co-Chairs

### Preamble

The Association for Specialists in Group Work (ASGW) is a division of the American Counseling Association whose members are interested in and specialize in group work. We value the creation of community; service to our members, clients, and the profession; and value leadership as a process to facilitate the growth and development of individuals and groups.

The Association for Specialists in Group Work recognizes the commitment of its members to the Code of Ethics and Standards of Practice (as revised in 1995) of its parent organization, the American Counseling Association, and nothing in this document shall be construed to supplant that code. These Best Practice Guidelines are intended to clarify the application of the ACA Code of Ethics and Standards of Practice to the field of group work by defining Group Workers' responsibility and scope of practice involving those activities, strategies and interventions that are consistent and current with effective and appropriate professional ethical and community standards. ASGW views ethical process as being integral to group work and views Group Workers as ethical agents. Group Workers, by their very nature in being responsible and responsive to their group members, necessarily embrace a certain potential for ethical vulnerability. It is incumbent upon Group Workers to give considerable attention to the intent and context of their actions because the attempts of Group Workers to influence human behavior through group work always have ethical implications. These Best Practice Guidelines address Group Workers' responsibilities in planning, performing and processing groups.

### Section A: Best Practice in Planning

#### A.1. Professional Context and Regulatory Requirements

Group Workers actively know, understand and apply the ACA Code of Ethics and Standards of Best Practice, the ASGW Professional Standards for the Training of Group Workers, these ASGW Best Practice Guidelines, the ASGW diversity competencies, the ACA Multicultural Guidelines, relevant state laws, accreditation requirements, relevant National Board for Certified Counselors Codes and Standards, their organization's standards, and insurance requirements impacting the practice of group work.

#### A.2. Scope of Practice and Conceptual Framework

Group Workers define the scope of practice related to the core and specialization competencies defined in the ASGW Training Standards. Group Workers are aware of personal strengths and weaknesses in leading groups. Group Workers develop and are able to articulate a general conceptual framework to guide practice and a rationale for use of techniques that are to be used. Group Workers limit their practice to those areas for which they meet the training criteria established by the ASGW Training Standards.

### A.3. Assessment

a. *Assessment of self.* Group Workers actively assess their knowledge and skills related to the specific group(s) offered. Group Workers assess their values, beliefs and theoretical orientation and how these impact upon the group, particularly when working with a diverse and multicultural population.

b. *Ecological assessment.* Group Workers assess community needs, agency or organization resources, sponsoring organization mission, staff competency, attitudes regarding group work, professional training levels of potential group leaders regarding group work, client attitudes regarding group work, and multicultural and diversity considerations. Group Workers use this information as the basis for making decisions related to their group practice, or to the implementation of groups for which they have supervisory, evaluation, or oversight responsibilities.

### A.4. Program Development and Evaluation

a. *Group Workers identify the type(s) of group(s) to be offered and how they relate to community needs.*

b. *Group Workers concisely state in writing the purpose and goals of the group.* Group Workers also identify the role of the group members in influencing or determining the group goals.

c. *Group Workers set fees consistent with the organization's fee schedule, taking into consideration the financial status and locality of prospective group members.*

d. *Group Workers choose techniques and a leadership style appropriate to the type(s) of group(s) being offered.*

e. *Group Workers have an evaluation plan consistent with regulatory, organization and insurance requirements, where appropriate.*

f. *Group Workers take into consideration current professional guidelines when using technology, including but not limited to Internet communication.*

### A.5. Resources

Group Workers coordinate resources related to the kind of group(s) and group activities to be provided, such as: adequate funding; the appropriateness and availability of a trained co-leader; space and privacy requirements for the type(s) of group(s) being offered; marketing and recruiting; and appropriate collaboration with other community agencies and organizations.

### A.6. Professional Disclosure Statement

Group Workers have a professional disclosure statement which includes information on confidentiality and exceptions to confidentiality, theoretical orientation, information on the nature, purpose(s) and goals of the group, the group services that can be provided, the role and responsibility of group members and leaders, Group Workers' qualifications to conduct the specific group(s), specific licenses, certifications and professional affiliations, and address of licensing/credentialing body.

### A.7. Group and Member Preparation

a. *Group Workers screen prospective group members if appropriate to the type of group being offered.* When selection of group members is appropriate, Group Workers identify group members whose needs and goals are compatible with the goals of the group.

b. *Group Workers facilitate informed consent.* Group Workers provide in oral and written form to prospective members (when appropriate to group type): the professional disclosure statement; group purpose and goals; group participation expectations including voluntary and involuntary membership; role expectations of members and leader(s); policies related to entering and exiting the group; policies governing substance use; policies and procedures governing mandated groups (where relevant); documentation requirements; disclosure of information to others; implications of out-of-group contact or involvement among members; procedures for consultation between group leader(s) and group member(s); fees and time parameters; and potential impacts of group participation.

c. *Group Workers obtain the appropriate consent forms for work with minors and other dependent group members.*

d. *Group Workers define confidentiality and its limits (for example, legal and ethical exceptions and expectations, waivers implicit with treatment plans, documentation and insurance usage).* Group Workers have the responsibility to inform all group participants of the need for confidentiality, potential consequences of breaching confidentiality and that legal privilege does not apply to group discussions (unless provided by state statute).

### A.8. Professional Development

Group Workers recognize that professional growth is a continuous, ongoing, developmental process throughout their career.

a. *Group Workers remain current and increase knowledge and skill competencies through activities such as continuing education, professional supervision, and participation in personal and professional development activities.*

b. *Group Workers seek consultation and/or supervision regarding ethical concerns that interfere with effective functioning as a group leader.* Supervisors have the responsibility to keep abreast of consultation, group theory, process, and adhere to related ethical guidelines.

c. *Group Workers seek appropriate professional assistance for their own personal problems or conflicts that are likely to impair their professional judgement or work performance.*

d. *Group Workers seek consultation and supervision to ensure appropriate practice whenever working with a group for which all knowledge and skill competencies have not been achieved.*

e. *Group Workers keep abreast of group research and development.*

## A.9. Trends and Technological Changes

Group Workers are aware of and responsive to technological changes as they affect society and the profession. These include but are not limited to changes in mental health delivery systems; legislative and insurance industry reforms; shifting population demographics and client needs; and technological advances in Internet and other communication and delivery systems. Group Workers adhere to ethical guidelines related to the use of developing technologies.

## Section B: Best Practice in Performing

### B.1. Self Knowledge

Group Workers are aware of and monitor their strengths and weaknesses and the effects these have on group members.

### B.2. Group Competencies

Group Workers have a basic knowledge of groups and the principles of group dynamics, and are able to perform the core group competencies, as described in the ASGW Professional Standards for the Training of Group Workers. Additionally, Group Workers have adequate understanding and skill in any group specialty area chosen for practice (psychotherapy, counseling, task, psychoeducational, as described in the ASGW Training Standards).

### B.3. Group Plan Adaptation

   a. *Group Workers apply and modify knowledge, skills and techniques appropriate to group type and stage, and to the unique needs of various cultural and ethnic groups.*
   b. *Group Workers monitor the group's progress toward the group goals and plan.*
   c. *Group Workers clearly define and maintain ethical, professional, and social relationship boundaries with group members as appropriate to their role in the organization and the type of group being offered.*

### B.4. Therapeutic Conditions and Dynamics

Group Workers understand and are able to implement appropriate models of group development, process observation, and therapeutic conditions.

### B.5. Meaning

Group Workers assist members in generating meaning from the group experience.

### B.6. Collaboration

Group Workers assist members in developing individual goals and respect group members as co-equal partners in the group experience.

### B.7. Evaluation

Group Workers include evaluation (both formal and informal) between sessions and at the conclusion of the group.

### B.8. Diversity

Group Workers practice with broad sensitivity to client differences including but not limited to ethnic, gender, religious, sexual, psychological maturity, economic class, family history, physical characteristics or limitations, **and** geographic location. Group Workers continuously seek information regarding the cultural issues of the diverse population with whom they are working both by interaction with participants and from using outside resources.

### B.9. Ethical Surveillance

Group Workers employ an appropriate ethical decision making model in responding to ethical challenges and issues and in determining courses of action and behavior for self and group members. In addition, Group Workers employ applicable standards as promulgated by ACA, ASGW, or other appropriate professional organizations.

## Section C: Best Practice in Group Processing

### C.1. Processing Schedule

Group Workers process the workings of the group with themselves, group members, supervisors or other colleagues, as appropriate. This may include assessing progress on group and member goals, leader behaviors and techniques, group dynamics and interventions; developing understanding and acceptance of meaning. Processing may occur both within sessions and before and after each session, at time of termination, and later follow-up, as appropriate.

### C.2. Reflective Practice

Group Workers attend to opportunities to synthesize theory and practice and to incorporate learning outcomes into ongoing groups. Group Workers attend to session dynamics of members and their interactions and also attend to the relationship between session dynamics and leader values, cognition and affect.

### C.3. Evaluation and Follow-Up

    a. *Group Workers evaluate process and outcomes*. Results are used for ongoing program planning, improvement and revisions of current group and/or to contribute to professional research literature. Group Workers follow all applicable policies and standards in using group material for research and reports.

    b. *Group Workers conduct follow-up contact with group members, as appropriate, to assess outcomes or when requested by a group member(s)*.

### C.4. Consultation and Training with Other Organizations

Group Workers provide consultation and training to organizations in and out of their setting, when appropriate. Group Workers seek out consultation as needed with competent professional persons knowledgeable about group work.

# F

# ASGW Principles for Diversity-Competent Group Workers

# PRINCIPLES FOR
# DIVERSITY-COMPETENT GROUP WORKERS

Approved by the ASGW Executive Board, August 1, 1998
Prepared by Lynn Haley-Banez, Sherlon Brown, and Bogusia Molina
Consultants: Michael D'Andrea, Patricia Arrendondo,
Niloufer Merchant, and Sandra Wathen

## Preamble

The Association for Specialists in Group Work (ASGW) is committed to understanding how issues of diversity affect all aspects of group work. This includes but is not limited to: training diversity-competent group workers; conducting research that will add to the literature on group work with diverse populations; understanding how diversity affects group process and dynamics; and assisting group facilitators in various settings to increase their awareness, knowledge, and skills as they relate to facilitating groups with diverse memberships.

As an organization, ASGW has endorsed this document with the recognition that issues of diversity affect group process and dynamics, group facilitation, training, and research. As an organization, we recognize that racism, classism, sexism, heterosexism, ableism, and so forth, affect everyone. As individual members of this organization, it is our personal responsibility to address these issues through awareness, knowledge, and skills. As members of ASGW, we need to increase our awareness of our own biases, values, and beliefs and how they impact the groups we run. We need to increase our awareness of our group members' biases, values, and beliefs and how they also impact and influence group process and dynamics. Finally, we need to increase our knowledge in facilitating, with confidence, competence, and integrity, groups that are diverse on many dimensions.

## Definitions

For the purposes of this document, it is important that the language used is understood. Terms such as "dominant," "nondominant," and "target" persons and/or populations are used to define a person or groups of persons who historically, in the United States, do not have equal access to power, money, certain privileges (such as access to mental health services because of financial constraints, or the legal right to marry, in the case of a gay or lesbian couple), and/or the ability to influence or initiate social policy because of unequal representation in government and politics. These terms are not used to denote a lack of numbers in terms of representation in the overall U.S. population. Nor are these terms used to continue to perpetuate the very biases and forms of oppression, both overt and covert, that this document attempts to address.

For the purposes of this document, the term "disabilities" refers to differences in physical, mental, emotional, and learning abilities and styles among people. It is not meant as a term to define a person, such as a learning disabled person, but rather in the context of a person with a learning disability.

Given the history and current cultural, social, and political context in which this document is written, the authors of this document are limited to the language of this era. With this in mind, we have attempted to construct a "living document" that can and will change as the sociopolitical and cultural context changes.

## The Principles

### I. Awareness of Self

A.  Attitudes and Beliefs

1.  Diversity-competent group workers demonstrate movement from being unaware to being increasingly aware and sensitive to their own race, ethnic and cultural heritage, gender, socioeconomic status (SES), sexual orientation, abilities, and religion and spiritual beliefs, and to valuing and respecting differences.

2.  Diversity-competent group workers demonstrate increased awareness of how their own race, ethnicity, culture, gender, SES, sexual orientation, abilities, and religion and spiritual beliefs are impacted by their own experiences and histories, which in turn influence group process and dynamics.

3.  Diversity-competent group workers can recognize the limits of their competencies and expertise with regard to working with group members who are different from them in terms of race, ethnicity, culture (including language), SES, gender, sexual orientation, abilities, religion, and spirituality and their beliefs, values, and biases. (For further clarification on limitations, expertise, and type of group work, refer to the training standards and best practice guidelines, Association for Specialists in Group Work, 1998; and the ethical guidelines, American Counseling Association, 1995.)

4.  Diversity-competent group workers demonstrate comfort, tolerance, and sensitivity with differences that exist between themselves and group members in terms of race, ethnicity, culture, SES, gender, sexual orientation, abilities, religion, and spirituality and their beliefs, values, and biases.

B.  Knowledge

1.  Diversity-competent group workers can identify specific knowledge about their own race, ethnicity, SES, gender, sexual orientation, abilities, religion, and spirituality, and how they personally and professionally affect their definitions of "normality" and the group process.

2.  Diversity-skilled group workers demonstrate knowledge and understanding regarding how oppression in any form—such as, racism, classism, sex-

ism, heterosexism, ableism, discrimination, and stereotyping—affects them personally and professionally.

3. Diversity-skilled group workers demonstrate knowledge about their social impact on others. They are knowledgeable about communication style differences, how their style may inhibit or foster the group process with members who are different from themselves along the different dimensions of diversity, and how to anticipate the impact they may have on others.

C. Skills

1. Diversity-competent group workers seek out educational, consultative, and training experiences to improve their understanding and effectiveness in working with group members who self-identify as Indigenous Peoples, African Americans, Asian Americans, Hispanics, Latinos/Latinas, gays, lesbians, bisexuals, or transgendered persons and persons with physical, mental/emotional, and/or learning disabilities, particularly with regard to race and ethnicity. Within this context, group workers are able to recognize the limits of their competencies and (a) seek consultation, (b) seek further training or education, (c) refer members to more qualified group workers, or (d) engage in a combination of these.

2. Group workers who exhibit diversity competence are constantly seeking to understand themselves within their multiple identities (apparent and unapparent differences), for example, gay, Latina, Christian, working-class and female, and are constantly and actively striving to unlearn the various behaviors and processes they covertly and overtly communicate that perpetuate oppression, particularly racism.

## II. Group Worker's Awareness of Group Member's Worldview

A. Attitudes and Beliefs

1. Diversity-skilled group workers exhibit awareness of any possible negative emotional reactions toward Indigenous Peoples, African Americans, Asian Americans, Hispanics, Latinos/Latinas, gays, lesbians, bisexuals, or transgendered persons and persons with physical, mental/emotional, and/or learning disabilities that they may hold. They are willing to contrast in a nonjudgmental manner their own beliefs and attitudes with those of Indigenous Peoples, African Americans, Asian Americans, Hispanics, Latinos/Latinas, gays, lesbians, bisexuals, or transgendered persons and persons with physical, mental/emotional, and/or learning disabilities who are group members.

2. Diversity-competent group workers demonstrate awareness of their stereotypes and preconceived notions that they may hold toward Indigenous Peoples, African Americans, Asian Americans, Hispanics, Latinos/Latinas, gays, lesbians, bisexuals, or transgendered persons and persons with physical, mental/emotional, and/or learning disabilities.

B. Knowledge

1. Diversity-skilled group workers possess specific knowledge and information about Indigenous Peoples, African Americans, Asian Americans, Hispanics, Latinos/Latinas, gays, lesbians, bisexuals, and transgendered people and group members who have mental/emotional, physical, and/or learning disabilities with whom they are working. They are aware of the life experiences, cultural heritage, and sociopolitical background of Indigenous Peoples, African Americans, Asian Americans, Hispanics, Latinos/Latinas, gays, lesbians, bisexuals, or transgendered persons and group members with physical, mental/emotional, and/or learning disabilities. This particular knowledge-based competency is strongly linked to the various racial/minority and sexual identity development models available in the literature (Atkinson, Morten, & Sue, 1993; Cass, 1979; Cross, 1995; D'Augelli & Patterson, 1995; Helms, 1992).

2. Diversity-competent group workers exhibit an understanding of how race, ethnicity, culture, gender, sexual identity, different abilities, SES, and other immutable personal characteristics may affect personality formation, vocational choices, manifestation of psychological disorders, physical "dis-ease" or somatic symptoms, help-seeking behavior(s), and the appropriateness or inappropriateness of the various types of and theoretical approaches to group work.

3. Group workers who demonstrate competency in diversity in groups understand and have the knowledge about sociopolitical influences that impinge upon the lives of Indigenous Peoples, African Americans, Asian Americans, Hispanics, Latinos/Latinas, gays, lesbians, bisexuals, or transgendered persons and persons with physical, mental/emotional, and/or learning disabilities. Immigration issues, poverty, racism, oppression, stereotyping, and/or powerlessness adversely impacts many of these individuals and therefore impacts group process or dynamics.

C. Skills

1. Diversity-skilled group workers familiarize themselves with relevant research and the latest findings regarding mental health issues of Indigenous Peoples, African Americans, Asian Americans, Hispanics, Latinos/Latinas, gays, lesbians, bisexuals, or transgendered persons and persons with physical, mental/emotional, and/or learning disabilities. They actively seek out educational experiences that foster their knowledge and understanding of skills for facilitating groups across differences.

2. Diversity-competent group workers become actively involved with Indigenous Peoples, African Americans, Asian Americans, Hispanics, Latinos/Latinas, gays, lesbians, bisexuals, or transgendered persons and persons with physical, mental/emotional, and/or learning disabilities outside of their group work/counseling setting (community events, social and political functions, celebrations, friendships, neighborhood groups, etc.)

so that their perspective of minorities is more than academic or experienced through a third party.

III. **Diversity-Appropriate Intervention Strategies**
 A. Attitudes and Beliefs
  1. Diversity-competent group workers respect clients' religious and/or spiritual beliefs and values, because they affect worldview, psychosocial functioning, and expressions of distress.
  2. Diversity-competent group workers respect indigenous helping practices and respect Indigenous Peoples, African Americans, Asian Americans, Hispanics, Latinos/Latinas, gays, lesbians, bisexuals, or transgendered persons and persons with physical, mental/emotional, and/or learning disabilities and can identify and utilize community intrinsic help-giving networks.
  3. Diversity-competent group workers value bilingualism and sign language and do not view another language as an impediment to group work.
 B. Knowledge
  1. Diversity-competent group workers demonstrate a clear and explicit knowledge and understanding of generic characteristics of group work and theory and how they may clash with the beliefs, values, and traditions of Indigenous Peoples, African Americans, Asian Americans, Hispanics, Latinos/Latinas, gays, lesbians, bisexuals, or transgendered persons and persons with physical, mental/emotional, and/or learning disabilities.
  2. Diversity-competent group workers exhibit an awareness of institutional barriers that prevent Indigenous Peoples, African Americans, Asian Americans, Hispanics, Latinos/Latinas, gays, lesbians, bisexuals, or transgendered members and members with physical, mental/emotional, and/or learning disabilities from actively participating in or using various types of groups, that is, task groups, psychoeducational groups, counseling groups, and psychotherapy groups or the settings in which the services are offered.
  3. Diversity-competent group workers demonstrate knowledge of the potential bias in assessment instruments and use procedures and interpret findings, or actively participate in various types of evaluations of group outcome or success, keeping in mind the linguistic, cultural, and other self-identified characteristics of the group member.
  4. Diversity-competent group workers exhibit knowledge of the family structures, hierarchies, values, and beliefs of Indigenous Peoples, African Americans, Asian Americans, Hispanics, Latinos/Latinas, gays, lesbians, bisexuals, or transgendered persons and persons with physical, mental/emotional, and/or learning disabilities. They are knowledgeable about the community characteristics and the resources in the community as well as about the family.
  5. Diversity-competent group workers demonstrate an awareness of relevant discriminatory practices at the social and community level that may be

affecting the psychological welfare of persons and access to services of the population being served.

C. Skills

1. Diversity-competent group workers are able to engage in a variety of verbal and nonverbal group-facilitating functions, dependent upon the type of group (task, counseling, psychoeducational, psychotherapy), and the multiple, self-identified status of various group members (such as Indigenous Peoples, African Americans, Asian Americans, Hispanics, Latinos/Latinas, gays, lesbians, bisexuals, or transgendered persons and persons with physical, mental/emotional, and/or learning disabilities). They demonstrate the ability to send and receive both verbal and nonverbal messages accurately, appropriately, and across/between the differences represented in the group. They are not tied down to one method or approach to group facilitation and recognize that helping styles and approaches may be culture-bound. When they sense that their group facilitation style is limited and potentially inappropriate, they can anticipate and ameliorate its negative impact by drawing upon other culturally relevant skill sets.

2. Diversity-competent group workers have the ability to exercise institutional intervention skills on behalf of their group members. They can help a member determine whether a "problem" with the institution stems from the oppression of Indigenous Peoples, African Americans, Asian Americans, Hispanics, Latinos/Latinas, gays, lesbians, bisexuals, or transgendered persons and persons with physical, mental/emotional, and/or learning disabilities, such as in the case of developing or having a "healthy" paranoia, so that group members do not inappropriately personalize problems.

3. Diversity-competent group workers do not exhibit a reluctance to seek consultation with traditional healers and religious and spiritual healers and practitioners in the treatment of members who are self-identified Indigenous Peoples, African Americans, Asian Americans, Hispanics, Latinos/Latinas, gays, lesbians, bisexuals, and transgendered persons and/or group members with mental/emotional, physical, and/or learning disabilities when appropriate.

4. Diversity-competent group workers take responsibility for interacting in the language requested by the group member(s) and, if not feasible, make an appropriate referral. A serious problem arises when the linguistic skills of a group worker and a group member or members, including sign language, do not match. The same problem occurs when the linguistic skills of one member or several members do not match. This being the case, the group worker should (a) seek a translator with cultural knowledge and appropriate professional background, and (b) refer to a knowledgeable, competent bilingual group worker or a group worker competent or certified in sign language. In some cases, it may be necessary to have a group

for group members of similar languages or to refer the group member for individual counseling.

5. Diversity-competent group workers are trained and have expertise in the use of traditional assessment and testing instruments related to group work, such as in screening potential members, and they also are aware of the cultural bias/limitations of these tools and processes. This allows them to use the tools for the welfare of diverse group members following culturally appropriate procedures.

6. Diversity-competent group workers attend to as well as work to eliminate biases, prejudices, oppression, and discriminatory practices. They are cognizant of how sociopolitical contexts may affect evaluation and provision of group work and should develop sensitivity to issues of oppression, racism, sexism, heterosexism, classism, and so forth.

7. Diversity-competent group workers take responsibility in educating their group members to the processes of group work, such as goals, expectations, legal rights, sound ethical practice, and the group worker's theoretical orientation with regard to facilitating groups with diverse membership.

## Conclusion

This document is the "starting point" for group workers as we become increasingly aware, knowledgeable, and skillful in facilitating groups whose memberships represent the diversity of our society. It is not intended to be a "how to" document. It is written as a call to action and/or a guideline and represents ASGW's commitment to moving forward with an agenda for addressing and understanding the needs of the populations we serve. As a "living document," the Association for Specialists in Group Work acknowledges the changing world in which we live and work and therefore recognizes that this is the first step in working with diverse group members with competence, compassion, respect, and integrity. As our awareness, knowledge, and skills develop, so too will this document evolve. As our knowledge as a profession grows in this area and as the sociopolitical context in which this document was written changes, new editions of these Principles for Diversity-Competent Group Workers will arise. The operationalization of this document (article in process) will begin to define appropriate group leadership skills and interventions as well as make recommendations for research in understanding how diversity in group membership affects group process and dynamics.

# References

American Counseling Association. (1995). *Code of ethics and standards*. Alexandria, VA: Author.

Association for Multicultural Counseling and Development. (1996). *Multicultural competencies*. Alexandria, VA: American Counseling Association.

Association for Specialists in Group Work. (1991). Professional Standards for Training of Group Workers. *Together, 20,* 9–14.

Association for Specialists in Group Work. (1998). Best Practice Guidelines. *Journal for Specialists in Group Work, 23,* 237–244.

Atkinson, D. R., Morten, G., & Sue, D. W. (Eds.). (1993). *Counseling American minorities* (4th ed.). Madison, WI: Brown & Benchmark.

Cass, V. C. (1979). Homosexual identity formation: A theoretical model. *Journal of Homosexuality, 4,* 219–236.

Cross, W. E. (1995). The psychology of Nigrescence: Revising the Cross model. In J. G. Ponterotto, J. M. Casas, L. A. Suzuki, & C. M. Alexander (Eds.), *Handbook of multicultural counseling* (pp. 93–122). Thousand Oaks, CA: Sage.

D'Augelli, A. R., & Patterson, C. J. (Eds.). (1995). *Lesbian, gay and bisexual identities over the lifespan*. New York: Oxford University Press.

Helms, J. E. (1992). *A race is a nice thing to have*. Topeka, KS: Context Communications.

*Reprinted with permission from Association for Specialists in Group Work.*

# G

# RESOURCES RELATED
# TO CHILDREN OF DIVORCE

## Readings for Counselors

Alpert-Gillis, L. J., Pedro-Carroll, J. L., & Cowen, E. L. L. (1989). Children of Divorce Intervention program: Development, implementation, and evaluation of a program for young urban children. *Journal of Consulting and Clinical Psychology, 57,* 583–587.

Barker, J., Brinkman, L., & Deardoff, M. (1995). Computer interventions for adolescent children of divorce. *Journal of Divorce and Remarriage, 23,* 197–217.

Bernstein, J. (1983). *Books to help children cope with separation and loss* (2nd ed.). New York: Bowker.

Berry, J. (1990). *Good answers to tough questions about divorce.* San Francisco: Children's Press.

Christensen, L., & DeVol, P. (1993). *The complete guide to elementary student assistance programs: Strategy, policy, and procedure.* St. Paul, MN: Hazelden.

Cowne, E. L., Hightower, A. D., Pedro-Carroll, J. L., & Work, W. C. (1990). School-based models for primary prevention programs with children. In R. P. Lorion (Ed.), *Protecting the children: Strategies for optimizing emotional and behavioral development* (pp. 133–160). New York: Haworth Press.

DeLucia-Waack, J. L. (1996). Children of divorce group work in the schools. In S. T. Gladding (Ed.), *New developments in group counseling* (pp. 27–28). Greensboro, NC: ERIC/CASS.

Farber, A., & Mazlish, E. (1980). *How to talk so kids will listen and listen so kids will talk.* New York: Avon.

Freeman, K. A., Adams, C. D., & Drabman, R. S. (1998). Divorcing parents: Guidelines for promoting children's adjustment. *Child & Family Behavior Therapy, 20,* 1–26.

Gardner, R. (1991). *The parents' book about divorce.* New York: Bantam Books.

Gendler, M. (1986). Group puppetry with school-age children: Rationale, procedure, and therapeutic implications. *The Arts in Psychotherapy, 13,* 45–52.

Gladding, S. T. (1998). *Counseling as an art: The creative arts in counseling* (2nd ed.). Alexandria, VA: American Counseling Association.

Hetherington, E. M. (1989). Coping with family transitions: Winners, losers and survivors. *Child Development, 60,* 1–14.

Hetherington, E. M., Stanley-Hagan, M., & Anderson, E. R. (1989). Marital transitions: A child's perspective. *American Psychologist, 44,* 303–312.

Hodges, W. (1986). *Interventions for children of divorce: Custody, access and psychotherapy.* New York: Wiley.

Kalter, N. (1990). *Growing up with divorce: Helping your child avoid immediate and later emotional problems.* New York: Free Press.

Landy, L. (1990). *Child support through small group counseling.* Boston: Kidsrights.

Lesowitz, M., Kalter, N., Pickar, J., Chethik, M., & Schaefer, M. (1987). School-based developmental facilitation groups for children of divorce: Issues of group process. *Psychotherapy, 24,* 90–95.

Liebmann, M. (1986). *Art therapy for groups: A handbook of themes, games, and exercises.* Boston: Brookline Books.

Morganett, R. S. (1990). *Skills for living: Group counseling for young adolescents.* Champaign, IL: Research Press.

Morganett, R. S. (1994). *Skills for living: Group counseling activities for elementary students.* Champaign, IL: Research Press.

Oppawsky, J. (1991). Utilizing children's drawings in working with children following divorce. *Journal of Divorce and Remarrige, 15,* 125–141.

Pedro-Carroll, J. L. (1985). *The Children of Divorce Intervention program: A procedures manual for facilitating a divorce support group for 4th–6th grade children.* Rochester, NY: University of Rochester Center for Community Study.

Pedro-Carroll, J. L., Alpert-Gillis, L. J., & Sterling, S. E. (1987). *Children of Divorce Intervention program: A procedures manual for conducting support groups with 2nd and 3rd grade children.* Rochester, NY: University of Rochester Center for Community Study.

Pedro-Carroll, J. L., & Cowen, E. L. (1987). The Children of Divorce Intervention program: Implementation and evaluation of a time-limited group approach. In J. P. Vincent (Ed.), *Advances in family intervention, assessment and theory* (Vol. 4, pp. 281–307) Greenwich, CT: JAI Press.

Smead, R. (1998). *Skills and techniques for group counseling with youth* [Video]. Champaign, IL: Research Press.

Sommers-Flanagan, R., Elander, C., & Sommers-Flanagan, J. (2000). *Don't divorce us: Kids' advice to divorcing parents.* Alexandria, VA: American Counseling Association.

Stern, M., & Newland, L. M. (1994). Working with children: Providing a framework for the roles of psychologists. *The Counseling Psychologist, 22,* 402–425.

Teyber, E. (1992). *Helping children cope with divorce.* New York: Lexington Books.

Wallerstein, J. S. (1983). Children of divorce: Stress and development tasks. In N. Garmezy & M. Rutter (Eds.), *Stress, coping and development in children* (pp. 265–302). New York: McGraw-Hill.

Wallerstein, J. S., & Kelly, J. B. (1980). *Surviving the breakup: How children and parents cope with divorce.* New York: Basic Books.

Wilcoxon, S. A., & Magnusom, S. (1999). Considerations for school counselors serving noncustodial parents: Premises and suggestions. *Professional School Counseling, 2,* 275–279.

Yauman, B. E. (1991). School-based group counseling for children of divorce: A review of the literature. *Elementary School Guidance & Counseling, 26,* 131–138.

### Books for Children

Ballard, R. (1993). *Gracie.* New York: Greenwillow Books.

Banks, A. (1990). *When your parents get a divorce: A kid's journal.* New York: Viking Press.

Berger, F. (1983). *Nuisance.* New York: Morrow.

Blume, J. (1972). *It's not the end of the world.* New York: Bradbury Press.

Boekman, C. (1980). *Surviving your parents' divorce.* Danbury, CT: Franklin Watts.

Boelts, M. (1992). *With my Mom, with my Dad.* New York: Pacific Press.

Boyd, L. (1990). *Sam is my half brother.* New York: Viking Press.

Brown, L. K., & Brown, M. (1986). *Dinosaurs' divorce.* Boston: Little, Brown.

Byars, B. (1982). *The animal, the vegetable, and John D. Jones*. New York: Delacorte Press.

Cain, B., & Benedek, E. (1976). *What would you do? A child's book about divorce*. Washington, DC: American Psychiatric Press.

Cantor, D. W., & Drake, E. A. (1983). *Divorced parents and their children*. New York: Springer.

Cleary, B. (1983). *Dear Mr. Henshaw*. New York: Morrow.

Cleary, B. (1991). *Strider*. New York: Morrow Junior Books.

Danzinger, P. (1982). *The divorce express*. New York: Delacorte Press.

Deaton, W. (1994). *A separation in my family: A child's workbook about parental separation and divorce*. New York: Hunter House.

Dolmetsch, P., & Shih, A. (Eds.). (1985). *The kids' book about single-parent families*. Garden City, NY: Doubleday.

Dragonwagon, C. (1984). *Always, always*. New York: Macmillan.

Field, M., & Shore, H. (1994). *My life turned upside down, but I turned it rightside up: A self-esteem book about dealing with shared custody*. New York: Center for Applied Psychology.

Gardner, R. (1970). *The boys' and girls' book about divorce*. New York: Science House.

Gardner, R. (1983). *The boys' and girls' book about divorce*. New York: Bantam Books.

Garigan, E., & Urbanski, M. (1991a). *Living with divorce—middle grades: Journal activities for personal growth*. New York: Good Apple.

Garigan, E., & Urbanski, M. (1991b). *Living with divorce—primary grades: Activities to help children cope with difficult situations*. New York: Good Apple.

Gilbert, S. (1982). *How to live with a single parent*. New York: Lothrop Lee & Shepard.

Girard, L. (1987). *At Daddy's on Saturday*. Niles, IL: Whitman.

Goth, B. (1969). *Where is Daddy?* Boston: Beacon Press.

Grunsell, A. (1990). *Divorce*. New York: Gloucester Press.

Hazen, B. S. (1978). *Two homes to live in: A child's eye-view of divorce*. New York: Human Sciences Press.

Hazen, B. S. (1983). *Two homes to live in*. New York: Human Sciences Press.

Heegaard, M. (1991). *When Mom and Dad separate: Children can learn to cope with grief about divorce*. Minneapolis, MN: Woodland Press.

Heegaard, M. (1992). *Drawing out feelings: Facilitator's guide for leading grief support groups*. Minneapolis, MN: Woodland Press.

Heegaard, M. (1993). *When a parent marries again: Children can learn to cope with family change*. Minneapolis, MN: Woodland Press.

Ives, S. (1985). *The divorce workbook: A guide for kids and families*. New York: Waterfront Books.

Ives, S., Fassler, D., & Lash, M. (1985). *The divorce workbook*. Burlington, VT: Waterfront Books.

Jayanti, A. (1981). *Silas and the mad, sad people*. New York: New Seed Press.

Kagy-Taylor, K., & Dansker, D. (1990). *All about change*. Cincinnati, OH: Beech Acres Aring Institute.

Kalb, J., & Viscott, D. (1976). *What every kid should know*. Boston: Houghton-Mifflin.

Kent, L. (1993). *Love is always there.* New York: Paulist Press.

Klass, S. S. (1986). *Page four.* New York: Scribner.

Klein, N. (1974). *Taking sides.* New York: Pantheon Books.

Krementz, J. (1984). *How it feels when parents divorce.* New York: Knopf.

Lansky, V. (1998). *It's not your fault, KoKo Bear.* Minnetonka, MN: Book Peddlers.

Lash, M. (1990). *My kind of family: A book for kids in single-parent homes.* Burlington, VT: Waterfront Books.

Leach, N., & Browne, J. (1992). *My wicked stepmother.* New York: Macmillan.

Lebowitz, M. (1989). *I think divorce stinks.* New York: CDC Press.

LeShan, E. (1986) *What's going to happen to me?* New York: Macmillan.

List, J. (1980). *The day the loving stopped: A daughter's view of her parents' divorce.* New York: Seaview Books.

Mayle, P. (1988). *Why are we getting a divorce?* New York: Harmony.

McLanahan, S. (1994). *Growing up with a single parent.* Cambridge, MA: Harvard University Press.

Norris, L. (1991). *D is for divorce.* New York: Health Communications.

Park, B. (1981). *Don't make me smile.* New York: Random House.

Park, B. (1989). *My mother got married (and other disasters).* New York: Random House.

Prokop, M. (1986a). *Divorce happens to the nicest kids: A self-help book for kids and adults.* Warren, OH: Alegra House.

Prokop, M. (1986b). *Kids' divorce workbook.* Warren, OH: Alegra House.

Ricci, I. (1980). *Mom's house, Dad's house: Making shared custody work.* New York: Collier Books.

Richards. A., & Willis, I. (1976). *How to get it together when your parents are coming apart.* New York: Bantam Books.

Rofes, E. E. (Ed.). (1981). *The kids' book of divorce, by, for and about kids.* Lexington, MA: Lewis.

Rogers, F. (1996). *Let's talk about it: Stepfamilies.* New York: Putnam.

Rogers, F. (1997). *Let's talk about it: Divorce.* New York: Putnam.

Simon, N. (1983). *I wish I had my father.* Niles, IL: Whitman.

Smith, D. (1974). *Kick a stone home.* New York: Harper Collins Children's Books.

Stinson, K. (1984). *Mom and Dad don't live together anymore.* Toronto, Ontario, Canada: Annick Press.

Swan-Jackson, A. (1998). *When your parents split up ... How to keep yourself together.* New York: Penguin Putnam Books.

Tyler, A. (1982). *Dinner at the homesick restaurant.* New York: Knopf.

Voight, C. (1983). *A solitary blue.* New York. Atheneum.

Zindel, P. (1975). *I love my mother.* New York: Harper & Row.

Zolotow, C. 1980. *If you listen.* New York: Harper & Row.

### Videos for Children

Aquarius Productions. *Healing wounded hearts* [Video]. Sherborn, MA: Author. (www.aquariusproductions.com).

Kids Rights. (1995a). *No fault kids: A focus on kids with divorced parents* [Video]. Charlotte, NC: Author. (1-800-892-KIDS).

Kids Rights. (1995b). *When Mom and Dad break up* [Video]. Charlotte, NC: Author. (1-800-892-KIDS).

Sunburst Communications. (1997). *If your parents break up ...* [Video]. Pleasantview, NY: Author. (www.sunburst.com).

### Materials for Children (Books, Puppets, etc.)

Clawson, C. (1995). *Self-within: Therapeutic puppets designed for professional use.* West Lafayette, IN: Author. (765-477-6193).

Cooper, J., & Martenz, A. (1993a). *Divorce I.* Warminster, PA: Mar*co Products.

Cooper, J., & Martenz, A. (1993b). *Divorce II.* Warminster, PA: Mar*co Products.

Cooper, J., & Martenz, A. (1993c). *Stepfamilies I.* Warminster, PA: Mar*co Products.

Cooper, J., & Martenz, A. (1993d). *Stepfamilies II.* Warminster, PA: Mar*co Products.

Epstein, Y. M., & Borduin, C. M. (1985). Could this happen? A game for children of divorce. *Psychotherapy, 22,* 770–773.

Games, T. (1997). *The divorce game.* Pleasantville, NY: Sunburst Communications. (www.sunburst.com).

Hudgins, M. (1993). *Feelings bingo game.* Warminster, PA: Mar*co Products.

The Ungame Company. (1987). *The ungame game.* Anaheim, CA: Author.

### Related Information About Children's Groups

Kids Rights. (1994). *Movin' on* [Game]. Charlotte, NC: Author. (1-800-892-KIDS).

### Information on the Internet

American Coalition for Fathers and Children. www.acfc.org.

Center for Divorce Education. www.divorce-education.com/mainbar.htm, www.divorce-education.com/banner2.htm.

Children and Divorce. www.aacap.org/factsfam/divorce.htm.

Children of Divorce: All Kinds of Problems. www.divorceform.org/all.html.

Children's Rights Council. www.vix.com/crc/home.html.

Divorce Central. www.divorcecentral.com.

Divorce and Children. ucl.broward.cc.fl.us/pathfinders/divorce.htm.

Divorce Course: A Parenting Course for Divorcing Couples. www.uinmind.com/index.htm.

Divorce Doesn't Go Away. www.4children.org/news/198divo.htm.

Divorce Info. www.divorceinfo.com.

Divorce Reality. www.4children.org/news/198ccon.htm.

Divorce Source: A Legal Resource for Divorce, Custody, Alimony, and Support. www.divorcesource.com.

Healing the Broken Heart: Children of Divorce. www.childrenofdivorce.com/index.html.

How Divorce Affects Children. www.vix.com/men/mitch/needless.html.

Neumann, G. The Sandcastles Program: Helping Children of Divorce Rebuild. www.sandcastlesprogram.com/index.html.

# H

# SESSION PLANNERS

# Sample of a 6-Session Group

| Session # | Topic | Session Title |
|---|---|---|
| Session 1 | Introduction | Introduction to Each Other and to the Group |
| Session 2 | Introduction | Lots of Children Have Parents Who Are Divorced |
| Session 3 | The Divorce Experience | How Divorce Happened in My Family |
| Session 4 | Feelings | Feelings About the Divorce |
| Session 5 | Parents' New Partners | I Tried to Get My Mom and Dad Back Together Again |
| Session 6 | Ending | Ending |

# 6-Session Group Planner

| Session # | Topic* | Session Title |
|---|---|---|
| *Session 1:* | Introduction | Introduction to Each Other and to the Group |

Notes:

Homework:

| *Session 2:* | Introduction | Lots of Children Have Parents Who Are Divorced |

Notes:

Homework:

*Session 3:*

Note to Leader: Remind members that there are 3 sessions left.

Notes:

Homework:

*Session 4:*

Notes:

Homework:

*Session 5:*

Note to Leader: Remind members that there is 1 session left. Assign homework to integrate what has been learned.

Notes:

Homework:

| *Session 6:* | Ending | Ending |

Notes:

*Chosen by leader on the basis of formal or informal assessment of children's needs.

# Sample of an 8-Session Group**

| Session # | Topic | Session Title |
|---|---|---|
| Session 1 | Introduction | Introduction to Each Other and to the Group |
| Session 2 | Introduction | Lots of Children Have Parents Who Are Divorced |
| Session 3 | The Divorce Experience | How Divorce Happened in My Family |
| Session 4 | The Divorce Experience | What Are Our Families Like? |
| Session 5 | The Divorce Experience | Our Families and Friends: Who Can We Talk To? |
| Session 6 | The Divorce Experience | Worries |
| Session 7 | The Divorce Experience | Is It My Fault? |
| Session 8 | Ending | Ending |

**Effectiveness currently being empirically investigated.

# 8-Session Group Planner

| Session # | Topic* | Session Title |
|---|---|---|
| *Session 1:* | Introduction | Introduction to Each Other and to the Group |

Notes:

Homework:

| *Session 2:* | Introduction | Lots of Children Have Parents Who Are Divorced |

Notes:

Homework:

*Session 3:*

Notes:

Homework:

*Session 4:*

Note to Leader: Remind members that there are 4 sessions left.

Notes:

Homework:

*Session 5:*

Notes:

Homework:

*Session 6:*

Notes:

Homework:

*Session 7:*

Note to Leader: Remind members that there is 1 session left. Assign homework to integrate what has been learned.

Notes:

Homework:

*Session 8:*      Ending                    Ending

Notes:

*Chosen by leader on the basis of formal or informal assessment of children's needs.

# Sample of a 12-Session Group

| Session # | Topic* | Session Title |
| --- | --- | --- |
| Session 1 | Introduction | Introduction to Each Other and to the Group |
| Session 2 | Introduction | Lots of Children Have Parents Who Are Divorced |
| Session 3 | The Divorce Experience | How Divorce Happened in My Family |
| Session 4 | The Divorce Experience | What Are Our Families Like? |
| Session 5 | The Divorce Experience | Our Families and Friends: Who Can We Talk To? |
| Session 6 | Feelings | Feelings About the Divorce |
| Session 7 | Feelings | The Emotional Process of Divorce |
| Session 8 | The Divorce Experience | Is It My Fault? |
| Session 9 | Legal Aspects | What Do All the Big Words Mean for Me? |
| Session 10 | Changes | Life Is Tough and Some Ways to Cope With It |
| Session 11 | Ending | Ending |
| Session 12 | Ending | What Have I Learned From This Group? |

# 12-Session Group Planner

| Session # | Topic* | Session Title |
|---|---|---|
| *Session 1:* | Introduction | Introduction to Each Other and to the Group |

Notes:

Homework:

| *Session 2:* | The Divorce Experience | Lots of Children Have Parents Who Are Divorced |
|---|---|---|

Notes:

Homework:

*Session 3:*

Notes:

Homework:

*Session 4:*

Notes:

Homework:

*Session 5:*

Notes:

Homework:

*Session 6:*

Note to Leader: Remind members that there are 6 sessions left.

Notes:

Homework:

*Session 7:*

Notes:

Homework:

*Session 8:*

Notes:

Homework:

*Session 9:*

Notes:

Homework:

*Session 10:*

Note to Leader: Remind members that there are 2 sessions left. Assign homework to integrate what they have learned.

Notes:

Homework:

| *Session 11:* | Ending | Ending |
|---|---|---|

Notes:

Homework:

| *Session 12:* | Ending | What Have I Learned From This Group? |
|---|---|---|

Notes:

*Chosen by leader on the basis of formal or informal assessment of children's needs.